John Logie Baird
and Television

John Logie Baird (1888–1946)

Pioneers of Science and Discovery

John Logie Baird and Television

Michael Hallett

PRIORY PRESS LIMITED

Other Books in this Series

SBN 85078 228 7
Copyright© 1978 by Michael Hallett
First published in 1978 by
Priory Press Ltd., 49 Lansdowne Place, Hove, East Sussex
BN3 1HF
Photoset in 12/14 Baskerville and
printed and bound in Great Britain by
Redwood Burn Limited, Trowbridge & Esher

Contents

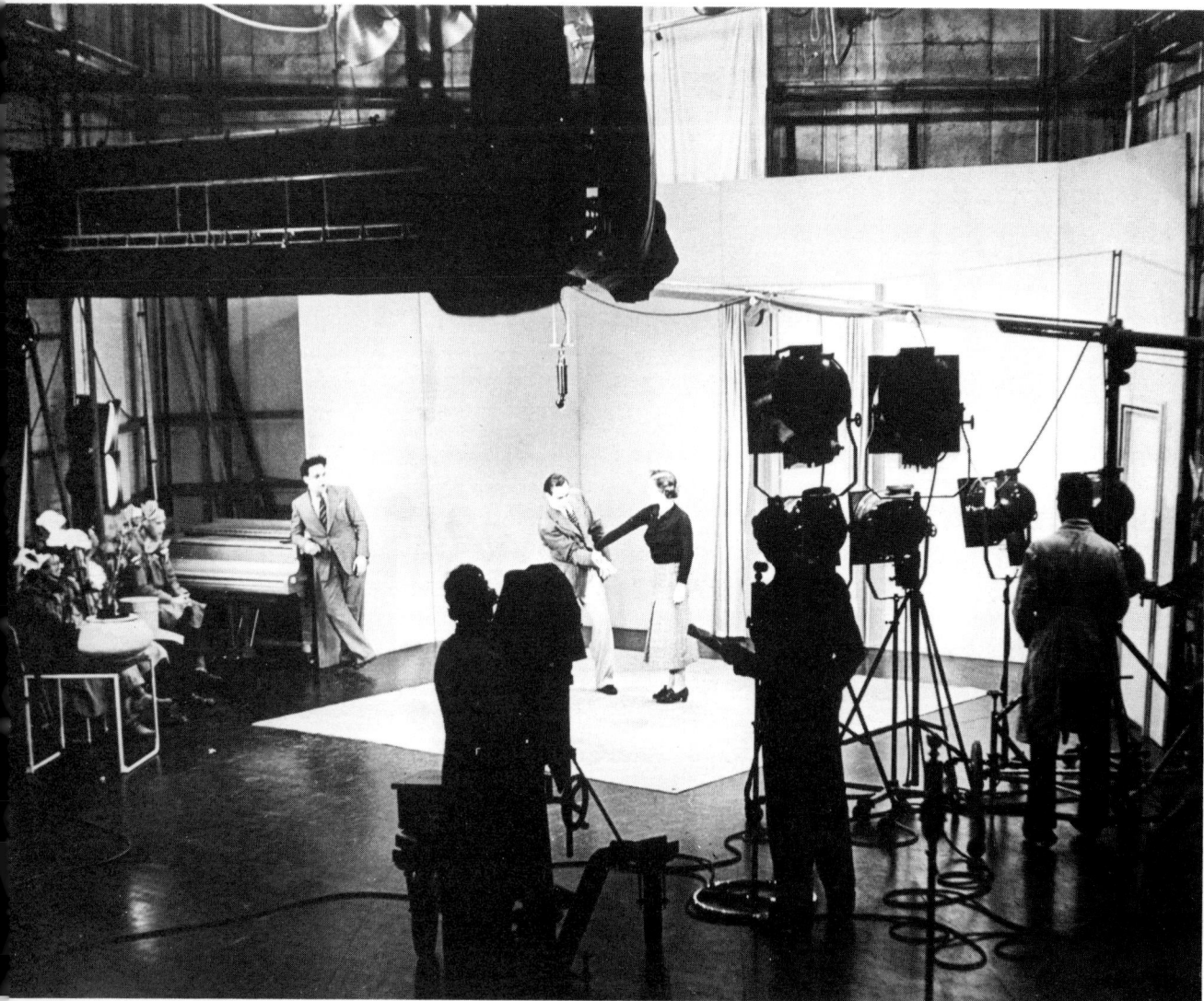

Above The BBC television service broadcasting on the art of self-defence from the Baird studio in 1936.

1 Introduction

John Logie Baird was a man of great courage and determination. All his life he suffered from bad health, but he had guts, an inventive mind and some commercial skill. Every time that he began to achieve success illness robbed him of it, but every time he recovered and started again. He was born four years after the first tentative step towards television had been taken. He was nine years old when the first crude demonstration of television took place in Russia. The *amplifying* valve, essential to television, was invented the year before that. When he started serious work on television in 1923, all the tools he needed had been developed. What he set out to achieve had at last become possible and he did it. He made television work.

Television is so much a part of our daily lives that it is easy to take it for granted, yet the story of how it came about is a fascinating one. The roots of the story stretch back through almost two thousand years to Lucretius, who studied the nature of electricity. Ideas and inventions from men working in Britain, America, France, Germany, Russia, Austria and others, began to come together. At the end of the 1800s the idea of distant vision, for that is what "television" means, began to seem a possibility. Many of these ideas that were found in the end to be essential to make television work, seemed at the time to have nothing to do with it. For example, in the summer of 1873, a young telegraphist called Joseph May, sitting in his office in Ireland, noticed something strange. This was in the days before wireless, and communications relied on the electric *telegraph* through which people could send messages to each other along a wire. Joseph May noticed that when the sun shone through his window onto his receiving set, it would not work properly, but as soon as he moved it out of the sun it was all right again. Not much to do with television, you might think, and yet it was a vital discovery.

Joseph May puzzled over this effect for a long time and at last he pinned the problem down to a *resistance* made of a metal called *selenium*. This resistance was meant to reduce the amount of electricity flowing through it. In the shade it worked perfectly but in sunlight it let too much electricity pass through and its resistance dropped. One of the first problems in making television work was how to "translate" light into electricity. May's discovery was to provide the answer in the *photo-electric cell*. If light is shone on a piece of selenium in this cell, connected to a battery, then the brighter the light the more current will flow. A pattern of changing light can be turned into a changing pattern of electricity.

Television, like the cinema, is an animated (moving) image. It depends on an effect called the "persistence of vision". It takes about one tenth of a second for an image to fade from the eye. If a sequence of pictures is flashed before your eyes faster than that you cannot see the difference between them; they appear to be moving. In the cinema you see a moving picture but, in fact, it is made up of twenty-four separate still pictures every second. On television there are twenty-five pictures each second. This effect has been known for a long time and in Victorian days many toys and games were made that were based on this principle. In the days before cinema some showmen made machines to show simple animated pictures to large audiences.

Right Samuel Morse (1791–1872), the American inventor of a code which could be sent along a wire by electricity. On paper, the code is written in dots and dashes.

About this time too, in the middle of the 1800s, the telegraph was becoming more sophisticated. In the days of Joseph May all that it could do was to send a simple "bleep" of electricity along a wire. Samuel Morse (1791–1872) invented his code of dots and dashes so that messages could be sent by this simple system. Soon *microphones* began to appear that could change the sound waves of a voice into electrical waves. These were sent along the wire to be changed back to sound at the other end by a *loudspeaker*. From this idea came the telephone.

9

People started to think "If we can send sounds along a wire, why not pictures?" The problem was that a wire could only handle a row of electrical signals, not a whole bunch of them at once. So it was necessary to break the picture up, to look at it a little bit at a time. Each bit must be translated into an electrical signal to be sent in a stream along the wire and put together at the other end. This was first successfully done by the Abbé Caselli who sent an electric picture from Amiens to Paris in 1862. He used a tiny

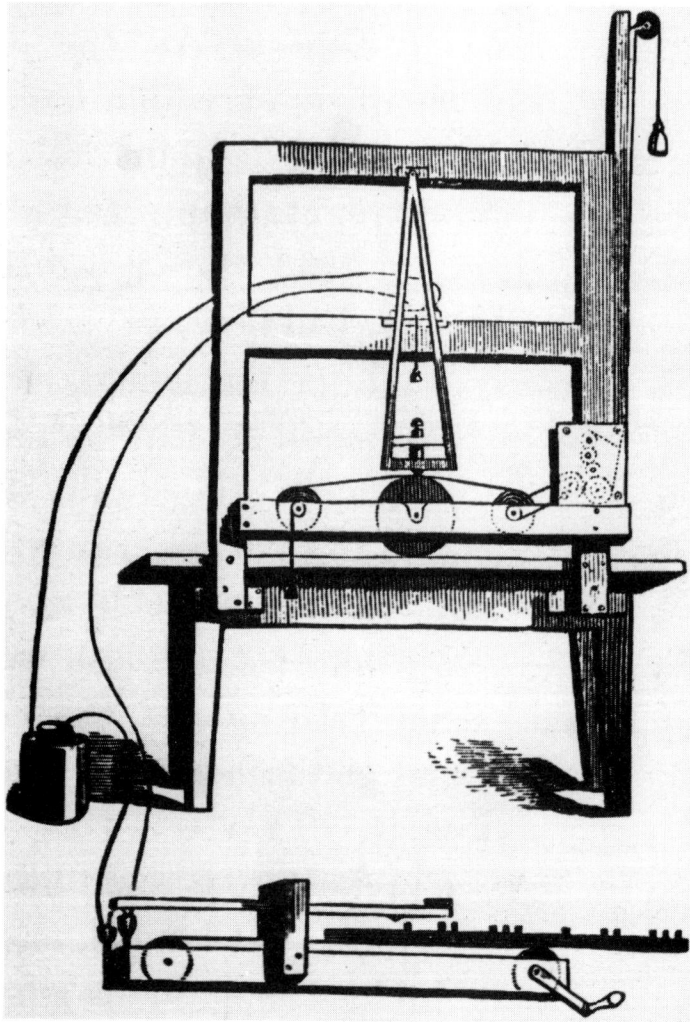

Left The original drawing on which Morse based his patent. The key at the bottom taps out the code, which is marked on the paper roll by a pen, held in the iron triangle, moved by an electro-magnet.

light bulb fixed to a carriage to *scan* the picture in a series of lines. As it moved, reflected light from the picture was picked up by a photo-electric cell for translation into electricity. This problem of scanning lies at the heart of the invention of television. Moving a lamp up and down the picture worked well enough for a single picture but it is much too slow for sending a sequence of pictures fast enough to make an apparently moving picture. In fact, in these early experiments it took about ten minutes to scan one single picture, whereas television would require at least sixteen pictures every second.

The first man to invent a practical way of scanning a picture fast enough was the German Paul Nipkow (1860–1940). In 1885 he patented his "spinning disc", which Baird used nearly forty years later. His idea was simply a disc with a spiral of holes cut in it. These were spaced so that as the disc spun in front of the picture each hole would trace out one line. The first hole would trace a line down the right-hand edge of

Right An early transmitted picture, sent in September 1863 by telegraph from Marseilles, France, to Paris. They called the process "electrotelegraphy".

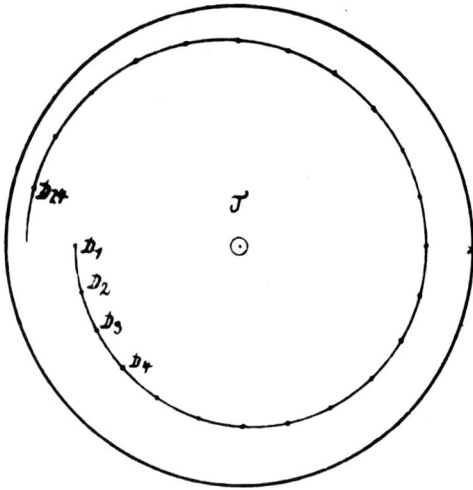

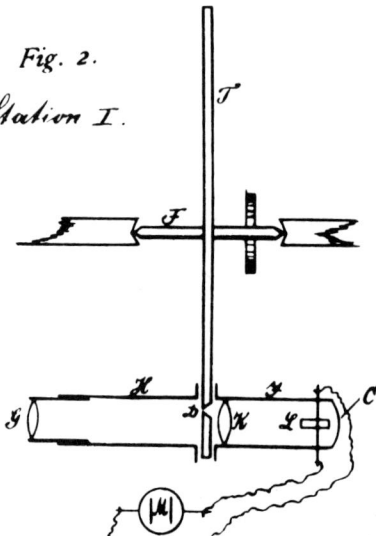

Left The original patent of January 1885 by Paul Nipkow for his spinning disc. The disc J, above, has 24 holes marked D, so the disc would scan a picture in 24 lines. Below, the disc J is seen side view. At the end of the tube is the photo-electric cell, C. Light is passed through the tube so the picture scanned by the disc is seen at U.

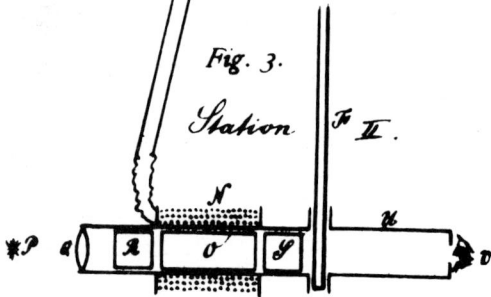

the picture. The next hole, being set slightly to the left of the first in the spiral, would trace a line to the left of the first. The third hole would trace a line to the left again and so on along the spiral until, in one turn of the disc, the whole picture had been scanned in as many lines as there were holes.

An even better idea came four years later from another German, Professor Weiller. He used a set of mirrors round a drum, each tilted away from the one next to it. As the drum turned, each mirror would cause a spot of light to sweep down the picture. The tilt of each mirror meant that each line was a little to the left of the previous one until, in one turn of the drum, the scan was complete.

Below An early cathode ray tube, first made by Karl Ferdinand Braun (1850–1918) in 1897. The source of electrons is on the left, then there is a plate with a small hole in it which makes a thin stream of electrons. There are two electromagnets, down and across, and then, the fluorescent screen.

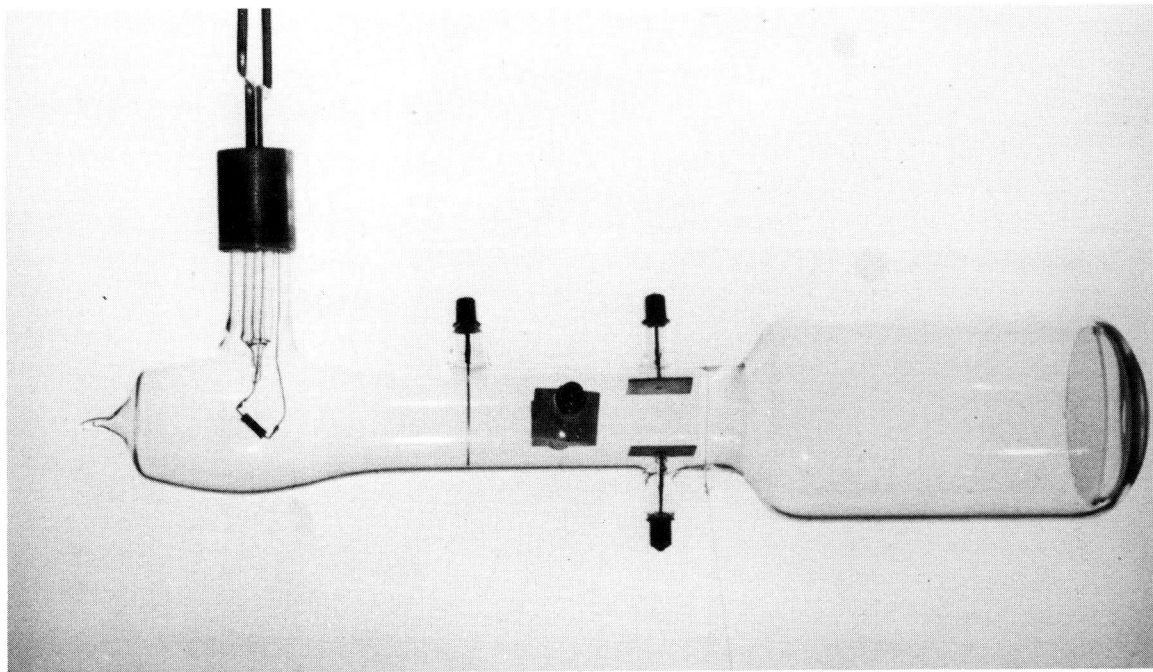

It was this mirror drum idea that was used in the world's first demonstration of television in 1907. Professor Boris Rosing (1869–1933) used two mirror drums, set at right angles to each other, to scan his subject. He scanned his picture both across and down, rather like noughts and crosses. He was only able to send black and white silhouettes of simple shapes, he could not send pictures in light and shade. Rosing sent the pictures from his mirror drum camera across his laboratory by wire. To receive them he used a *cathode ray tube*, very like the tube in a black and white television set. If a piece of wire is heated in a vacuum, it will give off streams of electrons, or *cathode rays*. These rays are invisible but some materials, called *phosphors*, can show them up because they glow when struck by the rays. These rays, like light, travel in straight lines but they can be moved about by magnets. Boris Rosing used a glass tube from which all the air had been removed. At one end was the wire that gave off the cathode rays. Next came a plate with a small hole in the middle from which a thin beam of cathode rays shone. Next came a magnet above the tube to control the movement of the beam up and down, then a magnet at the side to make the beam move left and right. Finally came the phosphor screen that glowed where the beam struck it.

With this arrangement he was able to make his beam of cathode rays sweep across and across the screen, each time getting lower and lower until it reached the bottom, when the magnets made it flick back to the top again ready for the next picture. Where the beam crossed a bit of the picture corresponding to the bright background the beam was full on and the screen glowed bluish-white. When the beam came to a bit corresponding to part of the image it switched off, leaving the screen dark, to switch on again when it emerged the other side.

Fig.1.

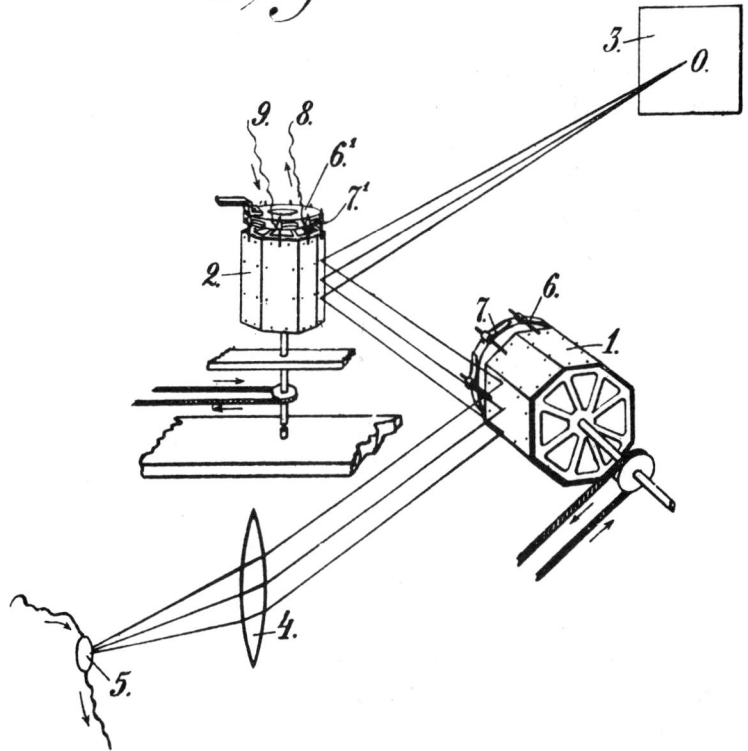

Fig. 2.

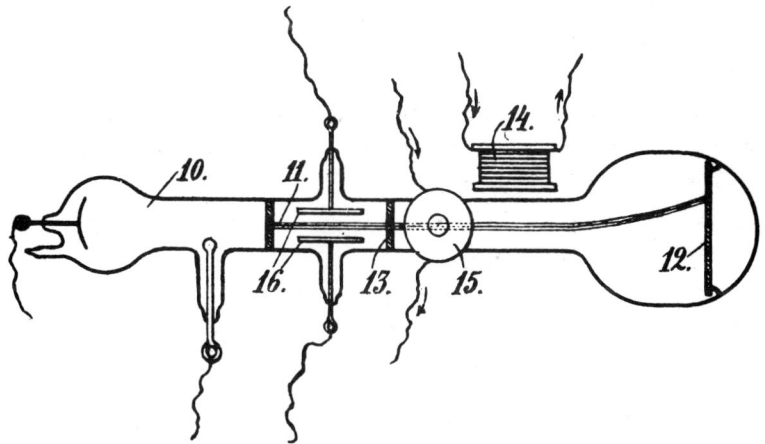

Right Rosings patent.
Above, the scanning
mirrors, and below, the
cathode ray tube. The
source of electrons is at 10. 15
and 16 are the electro-
magnets, and 12 is the
fluorescent screen that
shows them up.

Rosing could only send silhouette pictures because the amount of electricity that came from his photo-electric cells was too small to work the receiving tube. He did not have an *amplifier* to build up the strength of the electric current while being able to turn the picture from light to electricity. He did not know that the year before, in 1906, the key invention had been made across the world in America by Lee de Forest (1873–1961). He had invented the valve, that is the essential part of an amplifier. At the time few people recognized the tremendous importance of de Forest's work, but without it, wireless and television as we know them would not be possible. De Forest worked on improving his valve, which he called the "Audion" with no recognition outside scientific circles until the Great War broke out in 1914. The American army suddenly had a great need for communication over long distances and realized the importance of what he had achieved. The world was ready for wireless.

Towards the end of that war Revolution broke out

Below An Audion valve, invented by Lee de Forest in 1906. With this, an amplifier could be built to make an electric current strong enough to work the receiver without losing the signal.

in Russia and another of the great inventors in the story of television came to America. He was Vladimir Zworykin (b 1889) and he had been a pupil of Boris Rosing in Russia.

The mechanical systems based on the spinning disc and the mirror drum had a fatal flaw. To "paint" a well defined television picture a great amount of detail is needed in an extremely short time. Nothing mechanical could ever move fast enough to transmit the details. This was pointed out by A A Campbell Swinton (1863–1930) in 1908. He said that the way to get the speed would be by using electrons, which travel almost at the speed of light. He knew about the receiver end, for the sort of tube that Rosing used was well known. The snag was how to make an electronic camera, one that would convert the light of the picture into electricity by scanning it in lines by streams of electrons. The man who first saw how this could be done was Zworykin, who worked for the Westinghouse Brake Corporation. He filed his first application for a patent for an electronic camera, the "Iconoscope", in 1923. He did not get the money and facilities that he needed to perfect his idea until he joined RCA some years later. That is why the first practical electronic camera was built in England by EMI in 1932. The idea was Zworykin's and his Iconoscope and the EMI Emitron are very alike.

PHOTOGRAPHS BY TELEPHONE WIRE: THE COMING OF THE PICTOGRAM.

PHOTOGRAPHS BY THE AMERICAN TELEPHONE AND TELEGRAPH CO. SUPPLIED BY UNITED, SPORT AND GENERAL, AND TOPICAL.

TRANSMITTED BY TELEPHONE WIRE FROM CLEVELAND TO NEW YORK (NEARLY 400 MILES): A REMARKABLE PHOTOGRAPH OF THE HIGH LEVEL BRIDGE AT CLEVELAND, OHIO.

PRESS PORTRAITURE BY WIRE: A PHOTOGRAPH OF PRESIDENT COOLIDGE TRANSMITTED BY TELEPHONE WIRE.

SCIENCE is bringing into daily life a new wonder in the electrical transmission of pictures over long-distance telephone wires. On May 19, at Cleveland, Ohio, fifteen photographs were transmitted by wire to New York, nearly 400 miles, by a new process recently perfected by the American Telephone and Telegraph Company. The photographs, which showed street and river scenes, besides figure groups, were successfully reproduced in the "New York Times." The transmission of each picture took only four or five minutes, and one was reproduced 44 minutes after it was taken. The purpose of the [Continued opposite.

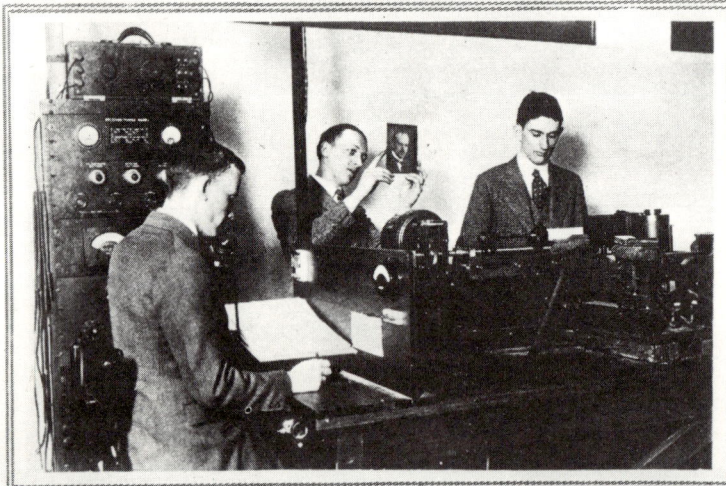

[Continued.)
test was to demonstrate to the Press the capabilities of the new method, and the results were regarded as placing it on a commercial basis. The system, developed by the engineers of the American Telephone and Telegraph Company and the Western Electric Company, is the outcome of work covering several years, and is simple, rapid, and accurate. The apparatus in its present form represents the association of many recent inventions, together with standard types of telephone and telegraph apparatus, re-adapted to this new use. The simplicity of the method is such that a positive transparency film supplied [Continued below.

HOW THE PHOTOGRAPHS TRANSMITTED OVER TELEPHONE WIRES FROM CLEVELAND, OHIO, WERE RECEIVED IN NEW YORK: THE RECEIVING-APPARATUS WITH THREE OPERATORS AT WORK, ONE EXAMINING A RESULT.

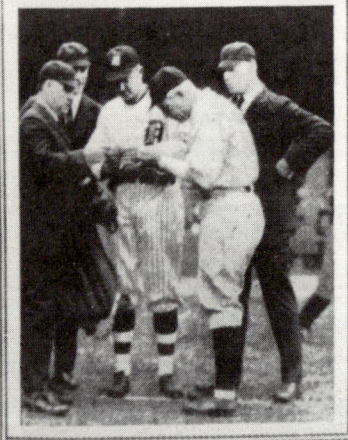

SENT OVER TELEPHONE WIRE NEARLY 400 MILES, LIKE THE OTHER ILLUSTRATIONS: A PHOTOGRAPH OF PRESIDENT AND MRS. COOLIDGE.

A GROUP PHOTOGRAPH TRANSMITTED BY TELE-PHONE WIRE TO NEW YORK: TWO BASEBALL

Left Report in the *Illustrated London News* of June 1924, explaining how press photographs can be sent by AT&T of USA.

Meanwhile, electronic methods such as we know today were on the horizon, but the believers in mechanical systems were hard at work. Two men stood out in 1925, the golden year of practical television. Real television, real moving pictures in light and shade, were achieved by two men, C F Jenkins in America and John Logie Baird in England. Historians cannot agree on who was first, but it is certain that neither knew of the other's work and both were true pioneers.

So the scene is set. An obscure Scottish electrician, whose life was filled with bad luck and dogged by ill health, took his place on the world stage. The dream of "distant electric vision" had become a reality. From then on, many others took part in the developments. Von Ardenna in Germany made great strides with mirror drum systems. Van Mihaly in Austria patented a mechanical camera called "Telehor", and the engineers of the Bell Telephone Company in America were full of inventive ideas. When the world's first regular public television service went on the air, however, it was the Baird system that televised the occasion.

Below The receiver built by Mihaly in Austria. The picture was built up of 180 lines.

2 *The Young Inventor*

Helensburgh is a town on the west coast of Scotland, where the weather is cold and damp. There, in a square grey stone house called "*The Lodge*" in Argyll Street, John Logie Baird was born on 13th August, 1888. His father, the Reverend John Baird, was Minister of the West Parish Church. He was a large, dark, stern man, with a big black beard and rather odd habits. He believed that the best time for a walk was the middle of the day and so every day he went out, returning at three o'clock for his lunch. This was awkward for Mrs Baird because John and the three elder children—Annie, Jean and James—had to have their lunch at the usual time, so she had to cook two lunches every day.

The family led a quiet life. A minister's pay was not much and the Reverend John Baird was a strict father and they were deeply religious. Few of the modern comforts had been invented. There was no electricity in *The Lodge*, no telephone and no wireless. The only way of getting about was to walk or ride. In later life, Baird recalled that he saw his first car when he was about eight years old. It was a clumsy thing with large wooden wheels, and it made a terrific clattering noise as it drove over the rough roads.

The young Baird was very imaginative. He was terrified of ghosts and as a small boy was often frightened to go to bed at night for fear of what might come. He used to tell of the time when he was only just tall enough to see out of the window; he looked out into the street and saw a very old man hobbling along with the aid of a stick. Baird ran from the window thinking he had seen himself an old man. He was not a healthy boy; he had a very weak chest. His first serious illness came when he was only two years old and throughout his life he suffered dreadfully from colds that drove him to bed for weeks on end.

Despite this handicap, Baird was an energetic boy, popular with his friends and a natural leader among them. At the age of six he went to a local school run by a Mr Porteous, who ran his school with a cane always tucked under his arm. Quite soon, Mr Porteous went bankrupt, but Baird was not saved for long. His next school was even worse, run by a Miss Johnston who also ruled her class with a cane. These years were perhaps the unhappiest of his life.

Outside school, however, his imagination led him to many experiments. His first great enthusiasm was for telephones, which were a new idea. He rigged up an exchange in his bedroom connected by wires across the streets to the houses of four of his friends.

Below The river Clyde at Helensburgh, near Glasgow, where Baird was born in 1888.

Before long the National Telephone Company found out about this and put a stop to it. He quickly showed a talent for electrical engineering and before long he had wired up *The Lodge* for electric light. He built his own generator run by a water wheel under the kitchen tap that fed a set of batteries.

His next passion was for photography. He found a camera and before long he set up a local photographic society. For a while this went well and absorbed his energy, but before long one of the

Below Baird aged 12. He took this self-portrait by remote exposure.

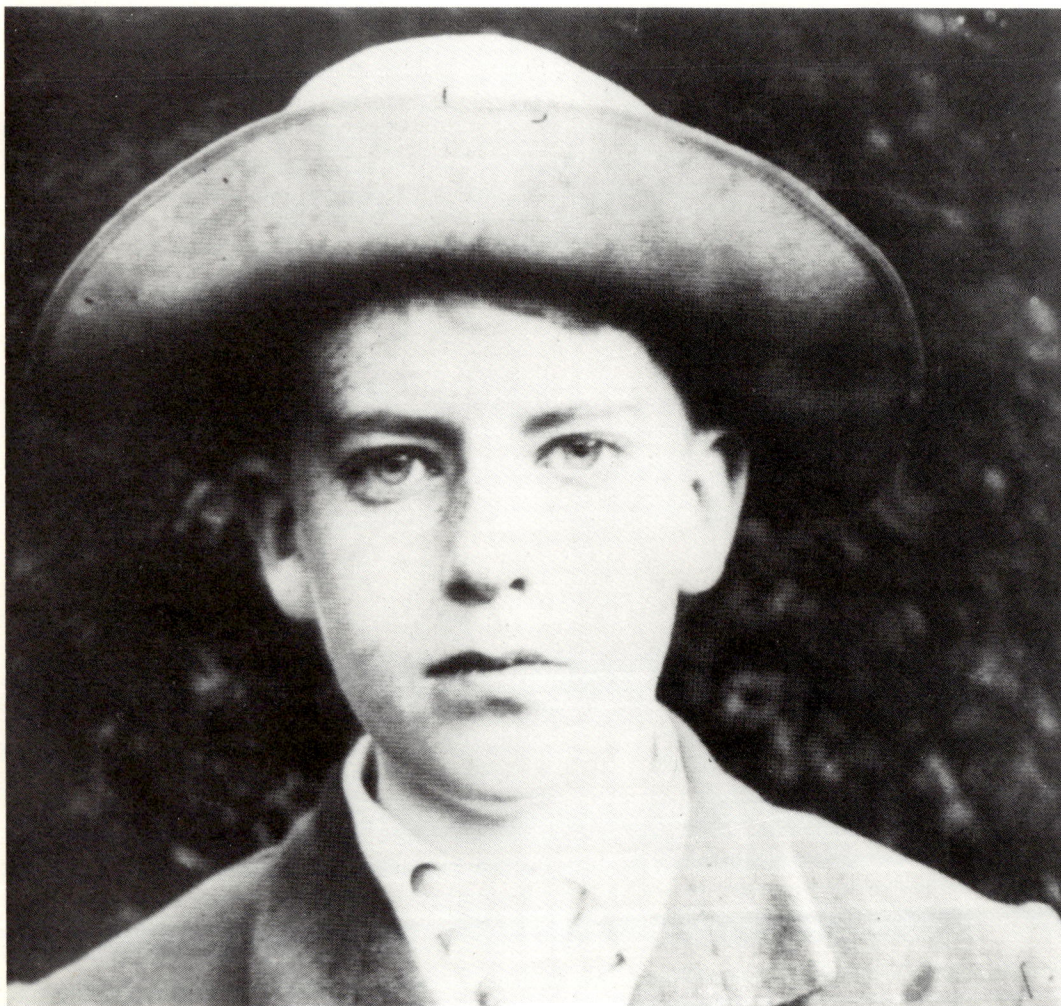

Above Baird and a friend in a three-wheeler car in The Trossachs, a mountainous area in Scotland, in 1906.

members came to complain that a man had boxed his ears for being rude. The society decided to take revenge, which Baird probably helped to plan. Their first move was to creep into his garden and catch his pigeons, which they sold to a local shop. Then they set their eyes on his prize tulips, and cut them down. This was too much for some of the members. They were afraid of what the authorities would say, and resigned. The club quickly passed a rule fining members for resigning, but the club faded away. Baird missed the club badly, both for the photography and the friendship.

At the age of eighteen Baird went to the Royal Technical College in Glasgow to study electrical engineering. One of his fellow students at the time was John Reith (1889–1971), who later became the first Director-General of the BBC. Baird gained his Diploma and Associateship, but he missed so much time because of constant ill-health that it took him five years instead of the usual three.

It was during this time that he learned of the discovery of Joseph May and the selenium cell. He was very keen to build his own apparatus, and used his cell in the kitchen. He was always in his mother's way, but she was very patient. He was trying to invent a way of making talking pictures. This was still before the First World War, when the cinemas showed silent films accompanied by a piano player. It was during these experiments that the idea of seeing by electricity first came to him. He did not pursue it at the time, but some ten years later he recalled these kitchen experiments. It changed his life, and made a great difference to ours.

His father wanted Baird to go into the Church, but he knew that this was not the life for him. Like all his family, he had been deeply religious as a boy but by now he was having serious doubts about religion. Electrical engineering was what interested him and he persuaded his father to let him go to Glasgow University. He studied for his BSc but in 1914 the First World War broke out and, like most young men, Baird went to the nearest Army Recruitment Office to join up. The interviews went well at first but then came the medical examination. Shivering, Baird took off his clothes. The doctor did not take long to examine him. As he was dressing, Baird saw what the doctor had written on his card: "Unfit for any service". Baird's heart sank.

He set out, very depressed, to find a job and took a place as an Apprentice Engineer in a local motor engineering works. He lived in squalid lodgings and the work was very hard and repetitive. He had to work very long hours and damaged his health by trudging through the dark, cold streets at five o'clock in the morning.

Right Royal Technical College, Glasgow. Baird studied electrical engineering here from 1906--1911, and it is here that he first met John Reith.

Then he got a job as a Superintendent Engineer at the Clyde Valley Power Company. He was on call day and night and when there was a breakdown he had to go out with a gang of workmen to find the fault and repair it. He spent many long nights in the cold and rain trying to persuade the men not to pack it up and go home. It was a miserable time for him and he remembered it as a time when he usually had bitterly cold feet. He tried to get promotion to a better job but

Left Baird at the Rutherglen sub-station of the Clyde Valley Power Company in 1915. His health suffered badly in this job.

his foreman told him he was away too much from sickness.

Even at the electricity company Baird was busy inventing. He knew that a diamond is only carbon that has been put under great pressure and heat. He took a rod of carbon and filed it to a narrow neck in the middle, so that it would heat up quickly when electricity was passed through it. He put this rod in an old iron pot and filled it with concrete. When the concrete had set, he connected the ends of the rod to the power station main output. There was a terrific bang and the main fuse blew, blacking out a large part of the town. Baird was ready for this and quickly had the fuses repaired. Lights came back but not before his superiors had come charging in to catch him in the act.

Baird realized that his job was ruining his health. He determined at all costs to get out and start up on his own. Remembering the miseries he had suffered from cold feet, he worked out a way of treating socks so that they would keep feet dry and warm. With his small savings he bought some socks and treated them himself in a small attic. Then he set off round the chemists' shops in Glasgow to sell the "Baird Undersock". He was quite successful and began to build up a useful little business, earning much more than he had been paid by the electricity company. He was a keen salesman. On one occasion he noticed that a big shop that had bought a dozen pairs of his socks had not put them on display. He rounded up all his friends and sent them one after the other into the shop to buy a pair. The shop quickly ordered more from Baird and displayed them where they could be seen easily.

For a while all went well, but then another of his disastrous colds kept him in bed for weeks. His business started to dwindle away, for he had no-one to help him.

He was attracted by the idea of the West Indies, where he thought that the hot climate would help his health. As soon as he was well again, he sold his business, became an agent to sell fancy goods, packed up his samples and took a ship to Port O'Spain in Trinidad. There he found the town full of agents with the same idea. Within a few weeks he went down with malaria. He lay in bed in his cheap lodgings, with very little money left and no job. He knew he would have to find a way to earn some money quickly. The idea came to him that on Trinidad grew both fruit and sugar. Both were cheap and plentiful, so why not start a jam factory?

As soon as he was well again he found just the place he was looking for—three bamboo huts in the Santa Cruz Valley. This was in the centre of the fruit growing region, some sixteen miles from Port O'Spain. He got some big copper vats and hired an assistant, a young Indian called Ram Roop. Together they filled the vats with fruit and sugar and started to boil them. It seemed as if every insect in Trinidad had smelled the jam. They came in great hordes, getting in Baird's hair and clothes and falling into the jam. This did not bother Ram Roop much, but it greatly upset young Baird. He kept going however and even kept a locust as a pet. For a year he made a modest success of his jam factory, but yet again his hopes were destroyed, for he went down with malaria. When he recovered, he packed jam into petrol tins and set off back to London to try to import his jam, but there were no offers. He finally sold the lot for fifteen pounds.

He tried yet again and made some money selling honey and fertilizer, but once more his health broke. A vicious cold kept him in bed for several weeks and his little business fell to pieces.

Back on his feet after six months, he was out of money and on the verge of despair. He kept on trying, however, and bought a load of soap. It was bad soap, but he was able to sell it so cheaply that it sold quickly. He set up a small company to import more soap and "Bairds Speedy Cleaner" was born. Soon he merged with his main rival, "Hutchinsons Rapid Washer" and success came quickly. It was not to last. He had a complete mental and physical breakdown. It was the most serious illness he had ever had. His doctor told him that he must leave the world of commerce, for his strength would not stand the strain, and ordered him to take a long rest on the south coast.

Baird therefore came to Hastings, late in 1922, a physically broken man at the age of thirty-four. He had no job and only £200 for which he had sold his soap company. It was an unpromising setting for one of the greatest developments in the history of invention.

3 Breakthrough

For four months Baird rested at Hastings, sharing an attic over a flower shop at No 8 Queen's Arcade with a childhood friend, Guy "Mephy" Robertson. Gradually his strength came back and he took long walks along the cliffs thinking as he walked. His great worry was how to earn a living. His little money was dwindling away and he had no prospect of a job. He had been on the edge of success several times. He made money with his socks, his soap and his jam, but every time his health had broken, and now he knew that he could not try again as a trader. He could see only one way: he must invent something. Day after day as he walked, he turned over ideas in his mind.

Then he began to think of the experiments he had done as a child in the kitchen at Helensburg with photo-electric cells. He realized that he had failed then because the electric current given out by this kind of cell was too tiny to work anything. There was then no way of amplifying this current. With mounting excitement he realized that such amplifiers now existed. The amplifying valve had been invented in America by Lee de Forest in 1906. He called it the "Audion", and military needs in the First World War had led to great strides in radio design. Surely with an amplifier, television must be possible?

The more he thought about it, the more he saw ways through the many problems. First, he would have to find a way to break the picture up, to look at it a tiny bit at a time so that his photo-electric cell could turn each bit into an electrical signal. This could be done by a disc cut with a spiral of holes in the way invented by Paul Nipkow in 1884. But what could he make the disc out of? It would have to be cardboard because he could not afford tools to make it of metal.

Above Baird's original television apparatus, now in the Science Museum, London. There is a replica in the Broadcasting Gallery of the Independent Broadcasting Authority. Bill is at A, B is the lensed scanning disc and C is a slotted disc for sampling the image.

Piece by piece in his mind he saw his machine. He knew that he could do it.

He hurried back to his attic as fast as he could and Guy Robertson listened in astonishment as his friend told him how he had invented a way of seeing by wireless. Robertson was doubtful about the whole thing; but he helped his friend to collect the weird assortment of bits and pieces that he wanted. An old tea chest served as a stand to mount the bits on. The lid of a hat box provided the disc and Baird carefully marked the spiral of holes and cut them out with a pair of scissors. A knitting needle served as a spindle and the motor from an electric fan was used to drive it. A photo-electric cell and some valves he got cheaply from an Army surplus store. He used dozens of torch batteries connected together to power his amplifier.

Baird worked feverishly and Robertson, still doubtful about the whole thing, watched as bit by bit the clumsy apparatus grew. Baird decided first to try to televise a simple cut-out cross shape to prove that he was on the right lines. On one side of the spinning disc he placed a bright light. This shone through the spiral of holes onto the cross behind it. Behind the cross he put his photo-electric cell and connected this through his amplifier to a neon lamp. The iines of his picture went from top to bottom, not across the screen as they do today, and the whole picture was made up of only 30 lines, whereas our present picture uses 625. As the disc spun, so spots of light swung

Below Diagram to show the parts of Baird's first apparatus. The slotted disc D replaced the disc at the front of the picture on page 31.

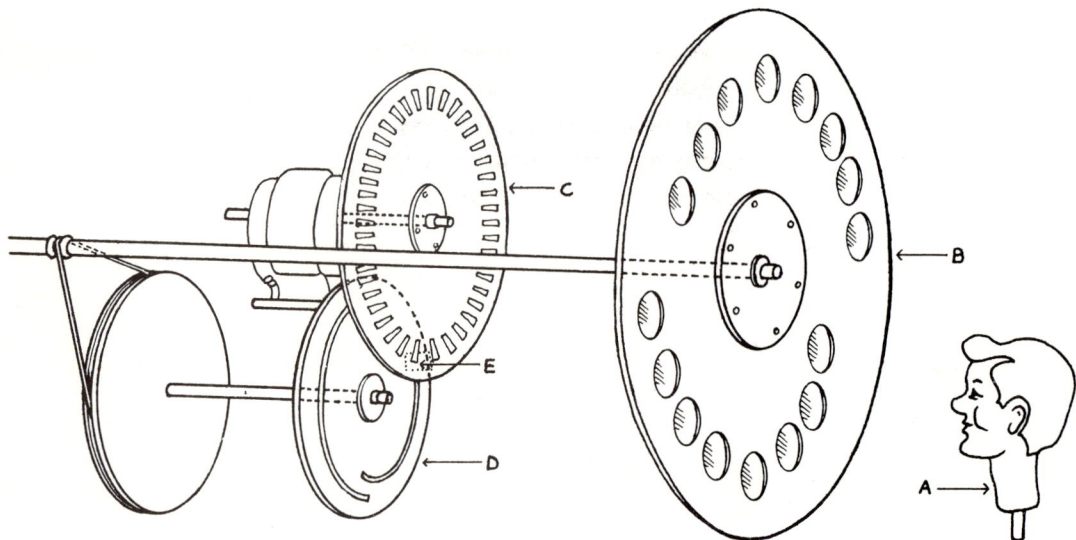

A - DUMMY'S HEAD (object to be transmitted)   B- REVOLVING DISC WITH LENSES

C&D - SLOTTED AND SPIRAL DISCS FOR SAMPLING   E - APERTURE THROUGH WHICH THE LIGHT PASSES TO THE PHOTO-ELECTRIC CELL

down the picture area. As each spot reached the edge of the cross the light was cut off from the photo-electric cell and the neon lamp went out. It went on again when the moving spot of light came out from the other side of the cross. Baird peered at the flickering neon through the edge of the disc and saw, faint and flickering, the picture of the cross. He had done it. He was on the right lines. His idea, born as he walked along the cliffs, actually worked.

Baird knew that his results and his apparatus were crude. He worked on, trying to improve the clarity of his results. By early 1924 he had separated the two halves of his arrangement, the camera and receiver. In his first experiments he used the same disc to scan the picture as a camera, and to show the picture as a receiver. Now he had two sets, he could transmit a picture from one set to the other. It was only a matter

Below The receiver end of the apparatus, once Baird had separated it into two parts, the transmitter and receiver, in 1924.

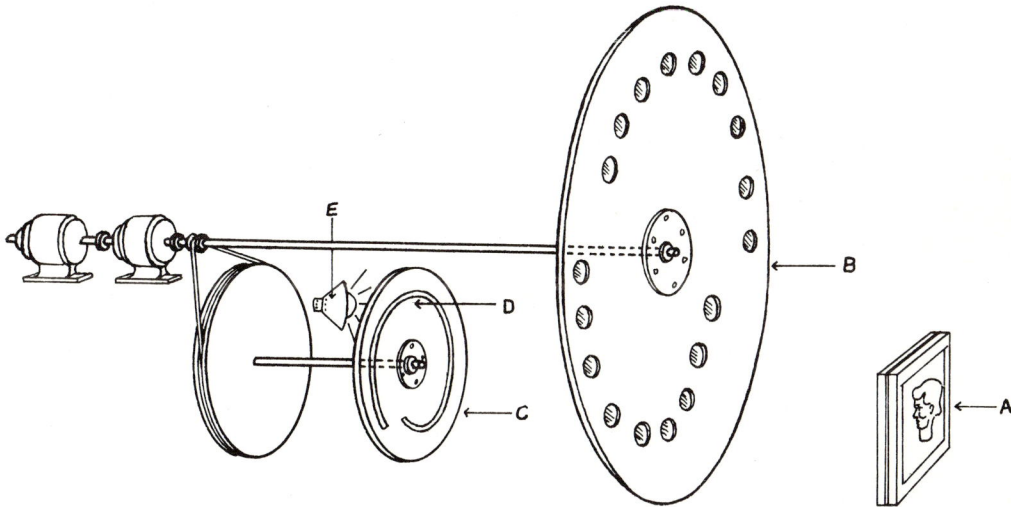

A - REPRODUCED IMAGE (on ground glass screen)   B - REVOLVING DISC WITH LENSES

C - ROTATING SPIRAL SLOT   D - APERTURE THROUGH WHICH THE LIGHT PASSES FROM THE
VARYING LIGHT SOURCE E

of three feet from the tea chest to the receiver by the wash basin, but it was a real start.

Now he was stuck; he needed to get better results. He needed a better amplifier, more sensitive photo-electric cells, he needed expensive motors that would run at constant speed. His cheap electric fan motors were a bit erratic. This was the snag; these things were expensive, and he had no money. He knew his equipment was not yet ready for public showing, but he had to have some financial backing.

He decided with regret that he would have to tell the world what he was doing and so he arranged a demonstration for the press. Not many people turned up but the *Daily News* wrote up the story and this had some useful results. Someone who read the story told Baird's father, who was very proud of his son's success and the family sent him what money they could

Left William Day, Baird's first financial backer. Day gave him help and encouragement in the early days.

find. Another man who read the story was a cinema owner called Will Day. He was ready for a gamble and bought a one-third share in Baird's invention for £200. Now he had some money to buy the equipment he needed. He spent nothing at all on himself, for he lived very simply and his clothes were worn and tattered; he spent every penny on his one passion—television.

His new equipment nearly led to disaster. To get the higher power that he needed he bought more and more batteries. One day something went wrong with the wiring. There was a terrific flash and bang and Baird had a severe electric shock. It did him no harm, but the next day the local newspapers reported the explosion. Mr Twigg, the landlord, heard of it and was very angry. He told Baird that his experiments must stop at once. Baird ignored him. There could be no thought in his mind of stopping. Mr Twigg insisted and served Baird with a Notice to Quit. Baird went back to London, without regrets and very determined. He was to meet Mr Twigg again, many years later, when a plaque was put up on that house in Hastings to commemorate the early days of television.

When Baird left London in 1922 he was desperately sick and had no idea what his future would hold. He returned with his equipment in 1924, in better health and with a purpose. He was beginning to make a name for himself and was totally dedicated to his dream.

4 *The First Real Television*

When Baird came to London early in 1925, his backer, Will Day, found him two attic rooms in Frith Street in Soho that he could use as a laboratory. Baird found himself lodgings in Ealing. He knew that he had made only a small start and that he had a long way to go before he could show that his system was good. He had proved that he was on the right lines, that his home-made bits and pieces could work, but he could only transmit simple shapes in black and white. He had to perfect his equipment until he could show pictures in light and shade, a recognizable human face, before he could attract real interest. He set up his transmitter in the attic using as his subject the battered head of a ventriloquist's dummy that he called Bill.

He tried to interest the Marconi Company, by now internationally famous in the field of wireless, but they did not think much of his invention. However, Gordon Selfridge, the owner of the famous store in Oxford Street, had heard of Baird and saw a possibility of good publicity for his store in television. He set out to find Baird and one cold March day he traced him to Frith Street and asked him to give personal demonstrations for three weeks at a Radio Show that Selfridge was arranging in his store. The fee was to be £20 a week and though the money was very welcome, Baird set greater value on the publicity.

The clumsy apparatus of wood and cardboard did indeed attract a lot of interest and much good came of it for Baird. A technical description was published in the important scientific journal *Nature*, but some of the popular papers voiced fears that this strange machine could be an invasion of people's privacy.

Some people even wondered if it could see through brick walls. Of more immediate importance, however, were two gifts of equipment. The General Electric Company gave Baird badly needed valves to the value of about £200 and the Hart Company gave him accumulators of the same value. His main backer, Will Day, was however beginning to doubt if he would ever see his money back and refused to put up any more.

The next few months were among the worst of his life. His money was virtually gone, his clothes were battered and lack of food began to affect his health. He tried hard to find backers but nobody took any interest in him. He floated a company, Television Limited, but no-one would buy any shares in it.

Hungry and nearly desperate he worked away in his attic. With the equipment that he had been given he was able to get a sharper picture of Bill, the dummy's head, but still it came over as a white shape, with no light and shade, no sign of eyes and nose, no tones of grey to make it look like a picture of a face. He knew that he had to demonstrate the televising of a recognizable face and that he had to do it quickly.

Below right A simple face shape which Baird transmitted in March 1925. He worked at improving his results until he had a more detailed image.

Below left Bill, the head of a ventriloquist's dummy. Baird used Bill as a subject in his early experiments.

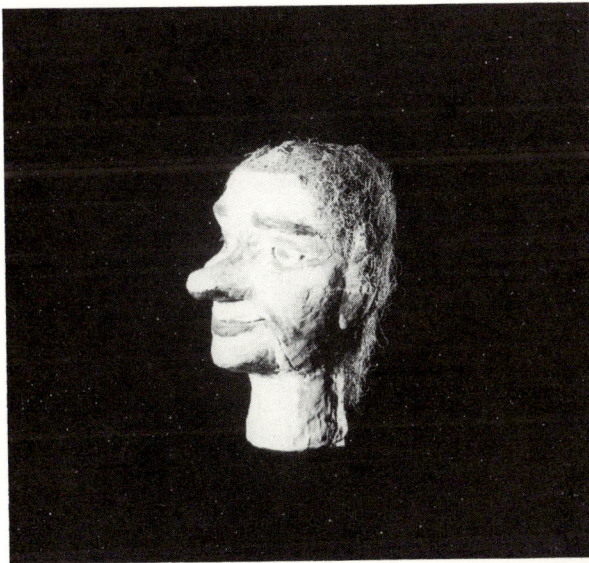

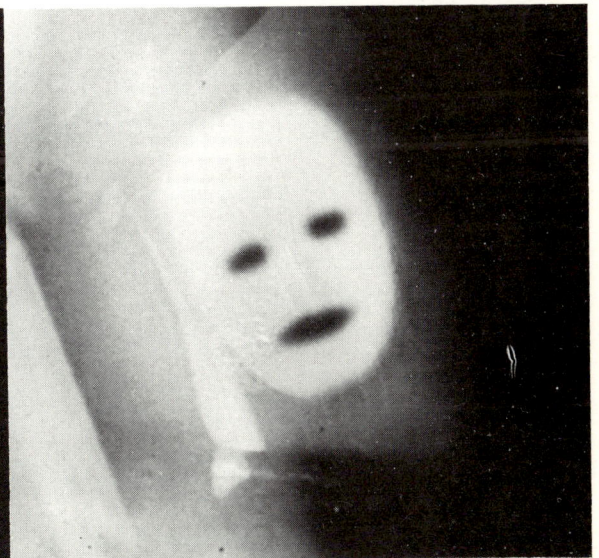

There were many others, particularly in America, working at problems similar to his own. Baird wanted to be first in the race, not only for himself, but because he was determined that the invention of television should be a British achievement.

It looked as if the work would have to be abandoned. With no money left even for food, let alone the equipment he needed, he was on the point of giving up. In desperation he swallowed his pride and appealed to his family in Helensburgh for help and their response was immediate. His father set up a fund to raise money for the work and his mother's family, who were prosperous ship owners, bought £500 of shares in Television Limited.

Relieved of his immediate anxieties, Baird set to work with fresh heart. He was sure that his problem lay in the optical side of his transmitter and this he completely rebuilt, but to no avail. The picture of Bill was still a white shape, better defined to be sure, but still featureless. Perhaps, he thought, the trouble lay in his photo-electric cell, that converted the light and shade of the picture into electricity. He built a new and more light-sensitive system and then, on 2nd October, 1925, it worked. For a long moment, Baird gazed at his apparatus, excitement welling up in him. There on the screen, in full light and shade, was the face of Bill. There was no doubt about it, after two years of desperate struggle he had done it. Now, instead of a dummy's head he had to have a live person in front of his camera. There was no time to lose.

On the first floor of that house in Frith Street, below Baird's attic, were the offices of Mr Cross, a solicitor. His office boy, William Taynton, was terrified when the wild figure of Baird burst into the office in a torrent of words, his excitement making his Scots accent almost incomprehensible. Frantically, Baird urged the boy upstairs and pushed him into a chair in a blaze of light in front of the camera. Baird dashed

38

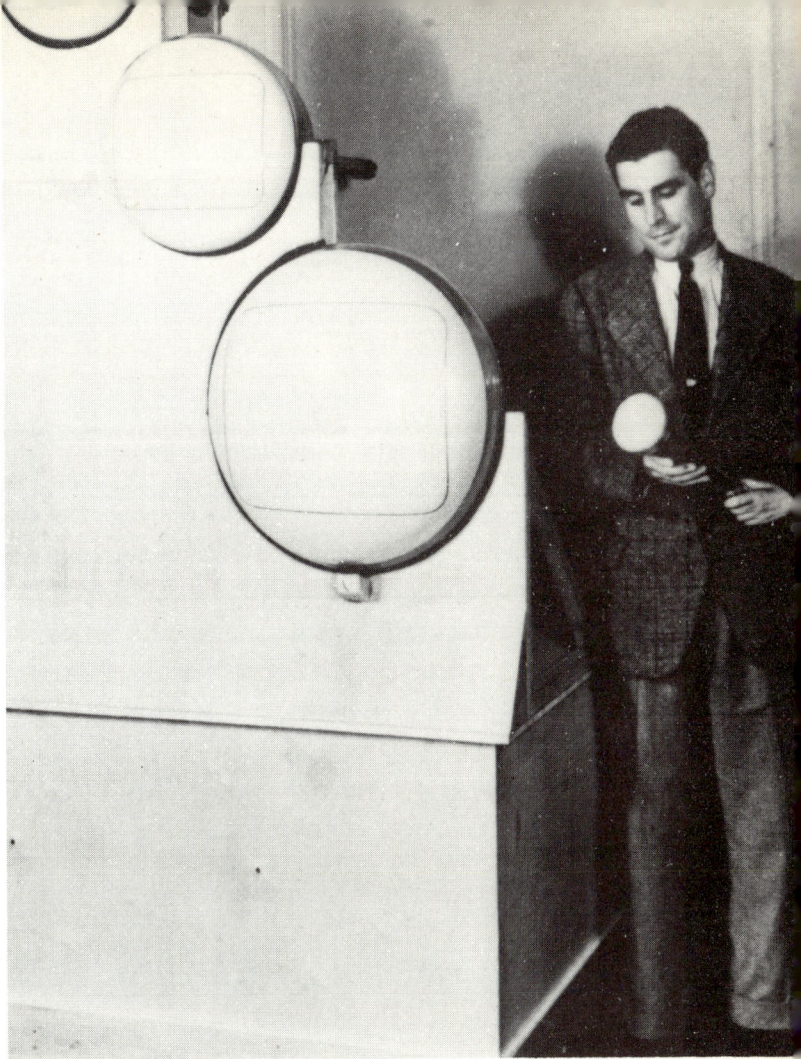

Right William Taynton, the first man ever to be televised. He is standing beside a display of cathode ray tubes, made by the Baird Television Company, at the Radio Show, Olympia, in 1939.

into the next room, where his receiver was set up, and there he stopped. His face fell. The screen was blank. He went back to the camera and there found that young Taynton, terrified of the whole scene, had backed as far away as he could from the blazing lights, out of the view of the camera. Baird tried to calm him down and gave him a tip to sit in the chair. Back at the receiver, Baird sighed with relief, for there on the screen was the face of William Taynton, the first man ever to be televised.

Mastering his excitement Baird sat down to some steady, methodical work. He had to check that the televising of William Taynton was no chance result, to be certain that his apparatus would work consistently, every time. When he was sure he had to move quickly for he was keenly aware of rivals in other countries, notably in America, who were, he felt sure, close behind him. After much thought he decided to invite members of the Royal Institution of Great Britain, one of the leading scientific societies of the day, to a demonstration in Frith Street.

On 27th January, 1926, helped by a journalist friend, W C Fox, he welcomed his guests, of whom over fifty turned up, crowding into every corner of the tiny rooms. The only newspaper invited to this very successful demonstration was *The Times*. In a report on 28th January the paper said:

"The image as transmitted was faint and often blurred but substantiated a claim that through the 'Televisor' as Mr Baird has named his apparatus it is possible to transmit and reproduce instantly the details of movement and such things as the play of expression on the face."

This report created a sudden flood of enthusiasm and swarms of journalists came to the laboratory to see for themselves. The American magazine *Radio News* sent a reporter across the Atlantic to interview him and news of his achievement spread wide and rapidly.

A chance meeting now brought Baird together again with his old rival in the soap business, Captain Hutchinson. Like Baird, Hutchinson was a dreamer but they did not get on too well together, for Hutchinson was a cautious man who wanted everything certain before any move was made, whereas Baird was much more ready to "have a go". He went out to give demonstrations wherever and whenever he could, even to the point of antagonizing some eminent scientists who did not approve of so much publicity-seeking. But Baird knew that he had to keep up public interest and he had to keep up financial back-

THE " TELEVISOR."

SUCCESSFUL TEST OF NEW APPARATUS.

Members of the Royal Institution and other visitors to a laboratory in an upper room in Frith-street, Soho, on Tuesday saw a demonstration of apparatus invented by Mr. J. L. Baird, who claims to have solved the problem of television. They were shown a transmitting machine, consisting of a large wooden revolving disc containing lenses, behind which was a revolving shutter and a light sensitive cell. It was explained that by means of the shutter and lens disc an image of articles or persons standing in front of the machine could be made to pass over the light sensitive cell at a high speed. The current in the cell varies in proportion to the light falling on it, and this varying current is transmitted to a receiver where it controls a light behind an optical arrangement similar to that at the sending end. By this means a point of light is caused to traverse a ground glass screen. The light is dim at the shadows and bright at the high lights, and crosses the screen so rapidly that the whole image appears simultaneously to the eye.

For the purposes of the demonstration the head of a ventriloquist's doll was manipulated as the image to be transmitted, though the human face was also reproduced. First on a receiver in the same room as the transmitter and then on a portable receiver in another room, the visitors were shown recognizable reception of the movements of the dummy head and of a person speaking. The image as transmitted was faint and often blurred, but substantiated a claim that through the "Televisor," as Mr. Baird has named his apparatus, it is possible to transmit and reproduce instantly the details of movement, and such things as the play of expression on the face.

It has yet to be seen to what extent further developments will carry Mr. Baird's system towards practical use. He has overcome apparently earlier failures to construct light sensitive cells which would function at the high speed demanded, and as he is now assured of financial support in his work, he will be able to improve and elaborate his apparatus. Application has been made to the Postmaster-General for an experimental broadcasting licence, and trials with the system may shortly be made from a building in St. Martin's-lane.

Right The report in *The Times* of 28th January, 1926; the only report of the first public demonstration of real television.

ing. He still had far to go and he still had rivals to beat. His pictures were dim, unsteady and often blurred and he worked with total absorption, often far into the night, slowly and painfully improving his results. Hutchinson disapproved, but he took over the business side, leaving Baird to concentrate on television. He brought in some more capital and more funds came from the family in Scotland and very soon Baird was able to move out of the cramped

41

rooms in Frith Street to more spacious accommodation in Monograph House, near Leicester Square. He even engaged an office boy, the first help that he had ever had, and later that year he took on a Mr Clapp as his Technical Assistant.

At Monograph House, Baird for the first time in his life had some money. After years of not being able to afford to eat enough he began to dine out at the best restaurants and thoroughly enjoyed the good life, until his doctor had to warn him off too much rich food.

Things were beginning to go a little better. Baird now had a studio on the top floor of Monograph House and a viewing room on the floor below. He applied to the Post Office for a transmitting licence and got it; the first ever television transmitter licence was "2 TV".

Although he was better off than before, he still needed more money. As his experiments proceeded, he needed more and more expensive equipment to make the next improvements. He was not an impressive figure, a small shabbily dressed man with large glasses and a shock of unmanageable hair. His equipment to the eye of the ordinary man was not very impressive. There were piles of bits and pieces and hopeless tangles of wire. It was small wonder that he found it difficult to persuade businessmen to invest in his ideas. The one thing that he had to offer was a monopoly; he was the only man who knew how to make television work. Hutchinson handled the business negotiations and at last he was successful. Agreement was reached that created the Baird Television Company Limited and capital could be raised. That night Baird and Hutchinson had a celebratory dinner, not realising that they were only just in the nick of time. The next morning the newspapers broke the news that the American Telegraph and Telephone Company had staged a spectacular show in New York called "Television at Last". Baird's monopoly had gone.

Left Baird in the Soho studio at Frith Street in March 1925. He is looking through his apparatus with the huge Nipkow disc in the middle.

5 *The World Wakes up to Television*

Now that there was a rival on the scene Baird knew that he had to work harder and faster than ever. He no longer had a monopoly of television and he had a healthy respect for the men in America. They had the support of a powerful corporation whereas Baird, with slender resources, was almost on his own. Nevertheless he was determined that Britain, which had been first in the field, should keep its lead. He had nothing to rely on but his own inventive genius. He set to work to press the development of television as far as he could.

One of the problems that bothered him about his system was the brilliant blaze of light that he had to use. Photo-electric cells were not very sensitive and light reached them through small holes in his disc, so he had to flood his subject with bright light. It was most uncomfortable for them, both from the brightness and the heat. Brooding about this, he wondered if he could use infra-red light instead, which is invisible to the naked eye. His subjects would be able to sit in darkness. Unfortunately ordinary photo-electric cells were not sensitive to infra-red light. He was however able to invent a suitable cell and was delighted at how well it worked. He found that his camera could even "see" through fog.

He called this system "Noctovision" and in December 1926 he invited members of the Royal Institution to his house on Box Hill in Surrey for a demonstration. For this he chose the evening, when it was dark, and used car headlights to show what his camera could do. He made covers for the headlights out of thin sheets of horn, which cuts out ordinary light but through which infra-red light can pass. As his guests watched from the house they could see the car headlights moving along the road below them. At the appointed spot the driver stopped the car and fitted the horn covers to the headlights. To the watchers above the lights vanished but when they went indoors to the television set the lights could still clearly be seen on the picture. The Navy showed some interest in this system because it could see through fog. Ordinary light gets scattered in all directions by the droplets that make up the fog, but the redder the light the less it is scattered. Waves too red to be seen by the eye are only slightly affected by the fog. It was thought that this could help to avoid accidents at sea, but nothing much came of it in the end.

Baird next turned his mind to colour television. He knew that a picture in full colour could be built up from the three primary colours, red, blue and yellow. He cut a scanning disc not with one spiral of holes, such as he used for his ordinary pictures, but with three spirals of holes. Each of the three sets of holes he covered with a coloured filter, one in each of the primary colours. When he had made an identical disc for his receiver he set up his equipment and tried it out. It worked quite well. The colours were a bit unsteady and the picture was only one inch square but it was another "first" for British television. He decided to give it a public demonstration. He invited

Right Baird's scanning disc for early colour television. The holes were covered with colour filters.

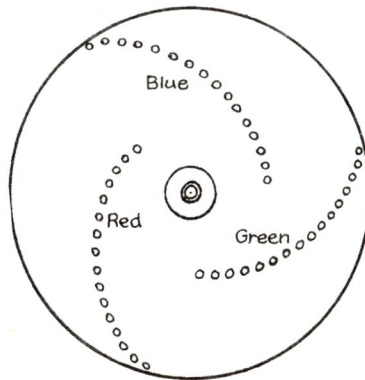

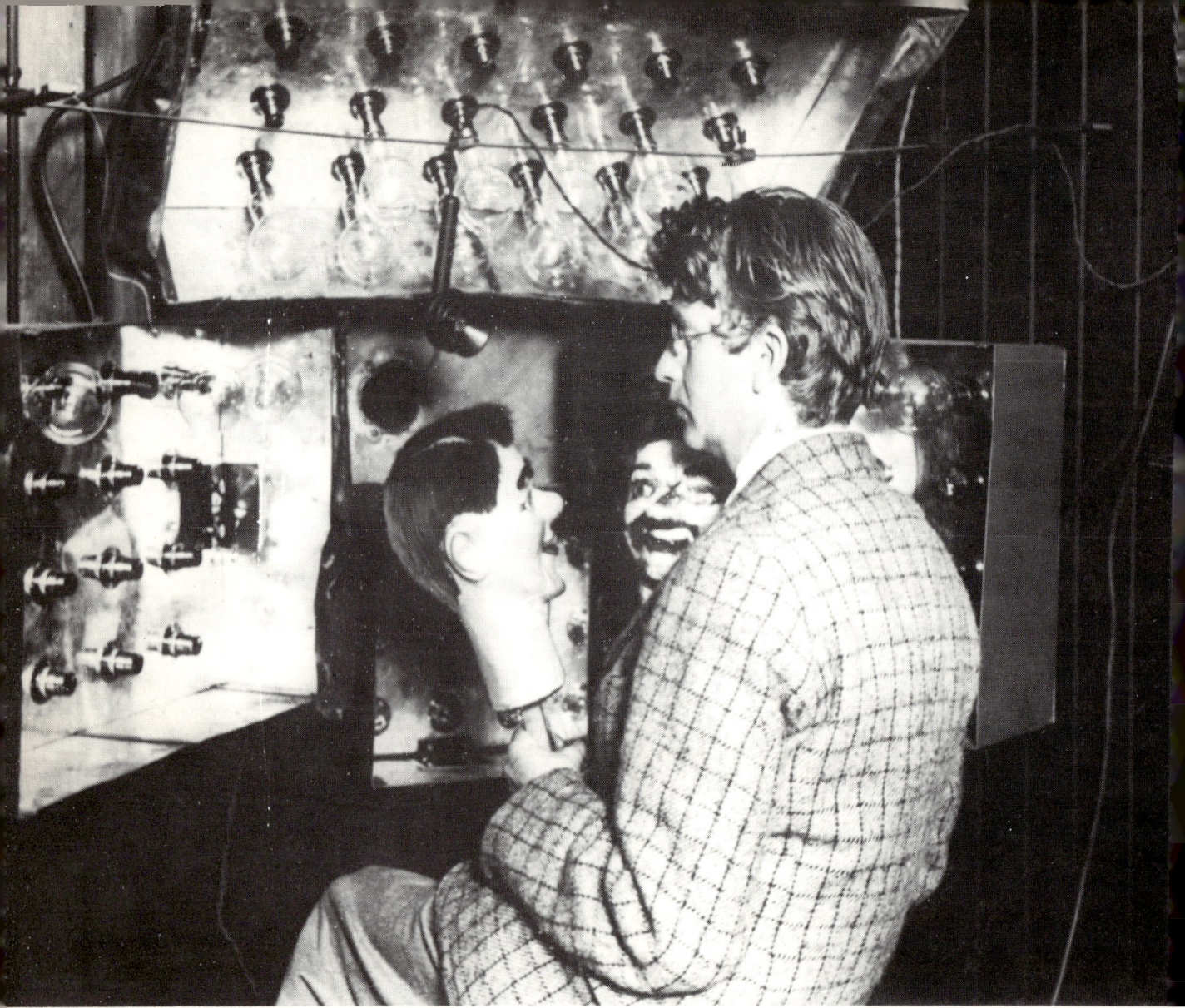

Above Baird in his studio holding two Bills. Note the sound microphone and banks of light bulbs; the blaze of light made his early subjects uncomfortable.

members of the British Association for the Advancement of Science and gave his demonstration in Glasgow, back in his home country.

In April 1927 came the news that the American Telegraph and Telephone Company had sent pictures by wire over a distance of 200 miles, from New York to Washington. He thought, "If distance makes headlines I can do better." The next month he transmitted pictures by telephone line from London to

Glasgow, a distance of 438 miles. Baird was still ahead!

Baird's name was becoming known to the public at large. More press reports appeared of progress not only by Baird himself but also by his American rivals. The eminent scientists who had been doubtful about the strange Scotsman with his extraordinary jumbles of bits and pieces, began to take him and his work more seriously. Indeed on one occasion he even found an elderly scientist who had disbelieved Baird's claims, lying on the floor peering up into a camera. Embarrassed at being discovered in such a position he explained that he had to satisfy himself that there was no trickery involved. Baird was delighted to explain the workings of his equipment and gained yet another convert.

Strains were beginning to develop between Baird and his old friend Hutchinson, who had so successfully managed the business side of the company. Hutchinson was by nature a cautious man who would have preferred Baird to wait and perfect each of his ideas before announcing them to the public. Baird, however, ever conscious of the need to keep one jump ahead of his rivals, was always keen to demonstrate as soon as he could be reasonably sure that his devices worked. At this time Baird met a man who was to figure largely in his affairs, Sidney Moseley.

Moseley was a financial journalist who knew the ways of the City intimately. Where Baird saw himself solely as an engineer, and hated the political and financial intrigues that had to go on, this was just the field that Moseley loved and understood. He quickly became a passionate supporter of Baird and the two men struck up a close friendship. Moseley took on the business side of things and left Baird free to concentrate on his work. He used his skill as a journalist to reply to Baird's critics and worked hard to ensure that reports of his successes were regularly published.

Now that the basic problems of television had been solved Baird knew that to make further progress he had to rely on the BBC, for the Corporation held a monopoly of broadcast transmission and it was in public transmission that the future lay. The year before, Baird had met the Chief Engineer of the BBC, Mr Kirke. He had been impressed by Baird's laboratory demonstrations and helped him to arrange a public broadcast. From the camera in Frith Street the signal had been sent by telephone line to the BBC studios and from there to the transmitter to be received by Baird back in Frith Street. They were successful in their way but the Corporation soon stopped them.

Baird was a little afraid of the Director-General of the BBC, John Reith. He was a tall Scot with a stern and powerful personality. He had been a fellow student of Baird's in Glasgow but even then he had been frightened of him. Moseley, however, was not frightened in the least. He loved this sort of battle and continued to persuade the BBC to take up regular transmissions. He lobbied members of Parliament, he wrote to the papers and he argued with the BBC.

The corporation's point of view was that Baird's system was not developed well enough for regular broadcasting. The pictures were dim, flickery and rather vague. The BBC had put a great deal of effort and research into broadcasting the highest possible quality of sound in their regular transmissions. Some experimental pictures were transmitted but it was years before Moseley's valiant efforts had any effect.

At the end of 1927 came another move for the Baird Company. They left Monograph House and moved to new and bigger premises a few hundred yards away in Long Acre, near Covent Garden. There Baird established his studio and laboratories and carried on with his researches. He happily left all the dealings of Board Meetings, financial affairs and similar problems to his friend Moseley.

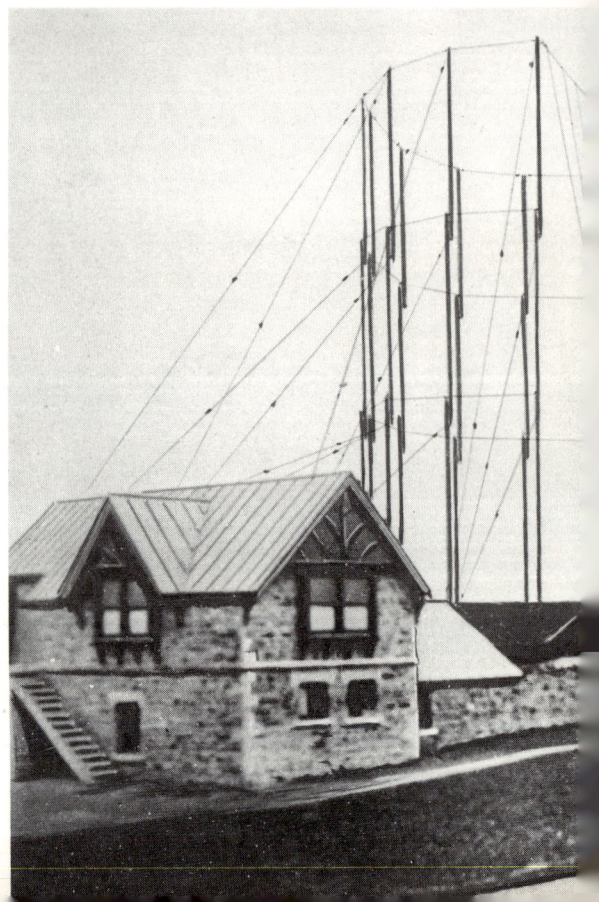

48

6 Television in Production

Left Sir John Reith (1889–1971), the Director-General of the BBC until 1938.

Below The transmitting station at Poldhu, Cornwall, where Marconi first sent messages in Morse to Newfoundland, early in the 1900s. Baird was determined to follow in Marconi's footsteps and send pictures across the Atlantic.

Baird was working on several different ideas early in 1928. He was absolutely committed to television and nothing existed for him but his work and his dreams. Although after so many years of hardship he now had a nice house at Box Hill, he worked for very long hours at his laboratory in Long Acre.

One success that meant much to him came in the cold days of February 1928. He had long wanted to follow the great man of radio, Marconi, who was the first to broadcast a radio message across the Atlantic. He wanted to be the first to send a picture to America, and his transmitter "2 TV" achieved it. He had sent his assistant, Mr Clapp, to America in late 1927, and he had succeeded in picking up both sound and vision; but the quality was very bad and they decided to say nothing about it at the time. Baird was determined however and this was a time at which he was making rapid strides. So in a few months, in February 1928, he set up his transmitter, "2 TV", at Coulsdon in Surrey, and sent Captain Hutchinson over to America with a new and improved receiver. Hutchinson set up his equipment and invited an American "ham" operator and a representative of Reuters, the world-wide press agency, to join him. Carefully he tuned in. Three thousand miles away, in Coulsdon, Baird lined up his camera and transmitter. Over the Atlantic Hutchinson and his American friends clearly saw a picture of Bill, the dummy's head. After a little while the screen was blank. Then appeared the face of Baird himself. The Americans watched with delight and the next day the news of this success was reported in the *New York Times*. This did much to make Baird famous in America.

Left Baird's picture recording machine, called Phonovision, of 1928. A needle cuts a groove in response to electrical impulses from the camera.

He was still working on several new developments but the main worry was still the tremendous amount of light that he had to use, which made his subjects uncomfortable. He was by now getting larger and clearer pictures, though his cameras could still only "see" the head and shoulders and not yet a full length figure. He was studying all the possible ways of making his cameras more sensitive, so that they could work with less light. At last, in the middle of the year, he achieved the target that he had set himself, a camera so sensitive that it would work by ordinary daylight. He built a studio on the roof of the building in Long Acre and everyone was more comfortable.

Another project that was on his mind was the possibility of recording his pictures. Sound records were made by a sharp needle cutting a groove in a disc of wax, responding to signals from a microphone. Baird found that by putting a camera in place of the microphone he could cut a groove that would correspond to the picture seen by the camera. His system divided the picture into only 30 lines, compared to the 625 lines used today. An ordinary gramophone record groove could "store" all the information needed. He found that to get good results it was necessary to keep the wax disc moving at the same speed as the disc in the camera. This he achieved quite simply by turning both of them by the

Right The National Radio
Exhibition at Olympia in
September 1928. Here Baird
displayed the prototype for his
factory-made television set—
the Televisor.

same electric motor.

Reports of Baird's work were regularly appearing
in the press due to Sidney Moseley, and more and
more people were seeing demonstrations. Some experimental broadcasts were going out from the BBC
transmitters although only a few sets existed to receive them. Baird thought there was enough public
interest for him to design a commercial television set
that could be made in a factory. The time was ripe, he
thought, to put television on the market.

He designed a set with this in mind and demonstrated it at the National Radio Exhibition in August
1928. It was a handsome thing in a large polished
wooden cabinet. Several famous actors and actresses
who visited the show were persuaded to give off-the-
cuff performances. One man who saw this set was
Percy Packman, at that time an engineer working for
the Plessey Company. He persuaded Baird that it
would be too heavy and that it needed some changes
in the mechanism. Baird agreed that Packman
should make one up to see how his ideas worked.

51

Packman and his colleagues at Plessey worked out the details and produced two hand-made models. One was given to Baird and Packman himself kept the other to check reception. What happened to Baird's one is not known but Packman's one, still in working order, survives to this day in the Broadcasting Gallery of the Independent Broadcasting Authority. Baird was impressed by the neat design of this set in its light metal case, and as a result Plessey won the contract to make the world's first mass-produced television set, the famous Baird "Televisor".

Baird knew that to make any further progress he had to have some public trials of television and that meant he had to go to the BBC, for the Corporation held the monopoly of public transmission. The BBC had been broadcasting occasional tests for almost two years and felt that they had all the evidence they needed. They were justly proud of the very high standards of technical excellence that they had achieved in their sound broadcasting. The leading BBC engineers, notably Eckersley and Ashridge, were doubtful about the dim flickering pictures that Baird produced and understandably did not wish to commit the Corporation to his system, which was still in its early stages.

There was a good deal of argument. There were many who sneered at Baird but he also had many supporters. The shy, rather hesitant Baird was not the man to fight this battle in the highest levels of the BBC and the Government but his close friend and supporter Moseley was just the man for the job. He bombarded the newspapers, lobbied members of Parliament and did everything that he could to bring about public television.

As a result of their efforts the Postmaster General, Sir William Mitchell Thomson, visited Baird at the end of 1929 to see for himself. He had a long talk with the inventor and saw a demonstration of what

Below A Baird Televisor. The picture was made of 30 lines, scanned vertically by Nipkow disc. The Plessey Company built 1,000 of these sets between 1929 and 1931.

television could do and he was impressed with its possibilities. He pressed the BBC to start regular broadcasts but still they refused. A few months later a Government re-shuffle brought a new man, Lees-Smith, to the Post Office and he pressed the BBC hard. At last they agreed and on 30th September, 1929 the inaugural broadcast went out from Baird's studio in Long Acre in the presence of the President of the Board of Trade, William Graham. It was a great day for Baird, who felt that he had broken through another barrier and taken an important step forward in the development of television.

At the time of this important broadcast Baird reckoned that there were about thirty television sets in existence. He, the Post Office and the BBC had one each and there were about six of the Plessey built Televisors. The rest had been made by amateurs. The announcer for this programme was Sidney Moseley and as there was only one transmitter he had to speak first into a microphone and then duck into the view of the camera. It was not until the March of the following year that the BBC was able to provide a second transmitter, so that sound and pictures could be broadcast simultaneously. Baird took it all as a matter of course. "It's just another milestone", he told the press.

At about this time he made a pleasant trip back to Hastings. There he met again his old landlord Mr Twigg, who had made him leave the house after the time his experiments caused a loud explosion. It was a happy event for Baird, though Mr Twigg may have had mixed feelings. They unveiled a plaque that the Council had put up to commemorate the building where those early experiments had taken place.

By now yet another idea was bubbling in his ever-active mind; big screen television, a screen so big that you could set it up in a cinema or theatre. The spinning disc that was the heart of his television set clearly would not do, for a disc big enough to give a large picture would have been gigantic. He would have to devise another way of displaying his pictures. The idea that he took up was simply a mass of electric light bulbs. If you look at a newspaper photograph through a magnifying glass you will see that it is made up of hundreds of tiny dots. Baird aimed to do the same thing, with 2,100 light bulbs on a board six feet wide by three feet high. These were wired up so that as the scanning line swept down the picture a vertical line of bulbs would be switched on in turn. These glowed brightly for light spots in the picture and less brightly for darker spots.

It was a massive task of electrical engineering to fit and wire up the thousands of bulbs and he drove his assistants hard, but at last it was done. The massive machine could only handle pictures at the rate of twelve every second, about half the speed of a cinema film, and as a result the picture looked very flickery. To demonstrate his invention Baird set up his screen in the Coliseum Theatre in London and on 28th July, 1930 the curtains parted to show a programme from Baird's studio. In pushing this plan through to a public demonstration so quickly Baird knew that he was taking a risk. He had left himself little time to check and perfect his machine but he felt a desperate sense of urgency because his rivals in America were making rapid strides. He was extremely nervous before the show but in the event it was successful. The story goes that a man who had had too much to drink wandered into the theatre thinking that it would be an ordinary show. When he saw a close-up of Moseley's face on the giant screen he leaped to his feet and rushed from the theatre swearing that he would never touch another drop.

This show was a tremendous success and the newspapers wrote enthusiastically about it. It also brought Baird a new field of support from the world of entertainment. He was so pleased by reactions that he sent the equipment on tour to Berlin, Paris

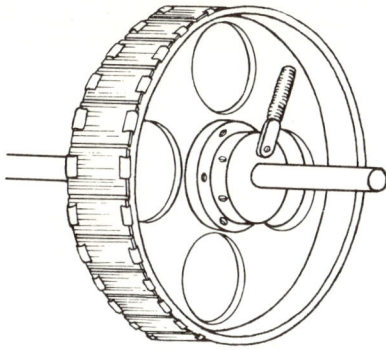

Above The mirror drum arrangement for scanning used by Baird after 1931.

Below A mirror screw, showing how many more strips of mirror can be fitted in a small space.

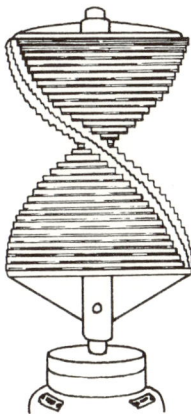

and Stockholm to advertise British television as widely as he could.

What to do next? Baird's restless imagination did not take long to think of a typically bold and risky plan. The BBC had been broadcasting live commentaries on the radio from sporting events. Why not take a television camera and mount the first ever television Outside Broadcast? He had developed a new kind of camera that was more sensitive than the previous ones with a spinning disc and given luck with the weather and a bright sunny day he reckoned that he could do it. He fixed on the Derby that would be run in June the next year, 1931, and set furiously to work.

In his new camera the spinning disc with its spiral of holes was replaced by a mirror drum, like the ones used by Professor Weiller and Professor Rosing. This was a drum on which a series of strips of mirror, one for each line, was mounted with each mirror tilted at a slight angle to the next one. This drum was mounted on a spindle and as a spot of light was shone on it the first mirror would cause a reflected spot to sweep down the picture. The next mirror, being slightly tilted, would cause its reflected spot to sweep down a little to the left of the first one. The spot from the third mirror would be a little to the left again and so on until each mirror had traced out a line and the whole set had covered the picture area.

As work on his Outside Broadcast van proceeded he approached the BBC and asked if they would broadcast the race. The Corporation finally agreed to help and the press was informed of the frequency of the transmission. The weather was good on the day of the race and Baird placed his camera near the winning post. He had only one camera so he decided to cover just the finish of the race. The programme was a success in a way but Baird was disappointed because the pictures were not good. Definition was poor and the picture flickered badly, but one could just see

55

the horses passing the post. Press reports the following day were quite good but much more importantly, the BBC was pleased. They still had their doubts about Baird's methods and equipment but were beginning to see the exciting prospect of a nationwide television service. They asked Baird to build a camera for them and put a small studio in Broadcasting House at his disposal. This was progress indeed. After many years of trying he was at last "inside the door" of the BBC.

Left C F Jenkins of America whose work was very similar to Baird's.

7 The Rival in Electronics

Despite his success in gaining entrance to the BBC, his company had troubles; it was going bankrupt. Television was still in a primitive state and there was no money coming in, indeed he even had to pay the BBC. The television sets were selling and bringing in some profits but these were very small compared to the high cost of research. Baird's backers were getting no return on their money and it was getting increasingly difficult to raise new capital. Baird was in despair, as he thought his work might have to stop. One of the few who did continue to back the venture in this difficult time was Isidore Ostrer, the millionaire head of the Gaumont-British cinema chain and as always there was Sidney Moseley, who bent all his financial skills to re-organizing the Company. Moseley was willing to part with some of his shares to raise money and America looked a promising place so in the autumn of 1931 he sailed for New York. There he met great interest in television but still a marked reluctance to put up hard cash. Time was running out and for two weeks Moseley worked frantically meeting people, talking, arguing and persuading. Finally from New York and London he raised enough money to take control of the Baird Company, whose direction was now firmly in Britain in the hands of Moseley and Ostrer. The BBC refused the offer of world control of Baird Television but no matter. The company was safe.

A small company, Baird TV Inc, was set up in New York. This company did not do very much and in September 1931 Baird was persuaded to go over and try to give it a boost. He sailed for New York in the liner *Aquitania*, which incidentally he had had a small hand in building as an apprentice twenty years before.

Baird was a shy man and did not like the enthusiastic greeting that met him in New York, a fantastic greeting such as only America can arrange. A bagpipe band was waiting at the quayside as the *Aquitania* docked to escort him through the streets to his hotel. This was too much for the quiet, sensitive man. He managed to escape and make his own way to his hotel, the *Waldorf*, where he was put out to learn that the Royal Suite had been booked for him. He found the black and gold bathroom of his suite overpowering, though he joked about it afterwards. His shyness also made him miserable when he had to attend a formal reception by the Mayor of New York, "Jimmy" Walker. Although being the man he was, he was not happy during the formalities, he was tremendously impressed with the warmth of his greeting.

Baird gave several demonstrations of his system and was pleased by the interest that they aroused. He succeeded in signing an agreement with the New York independent station WMCA to broadcast television pictures using his equipment, but by law this agreement could not take effect without the permission of the Wireless Commission. So off he went to Washington to see the Commission. He was used to the wigs and gowns and rigid rules of British courts so he was surprised to find how informal everything was. The Commission gave its approval to the agreement with WMCA, but the Radio Corporation of America appealed to the Federal Court on the ground that a foreign controlled company should not be allowed to broadcast in America. The court upheld this appeal and the agreement fell through. After three months in America it seemed that he had achieved nothing. Certainly the Board of Directors of the English company thought so. Baird was the visionary, the dreamer of the great things that could be, but they were hard-headed businessmen and they wanted results.

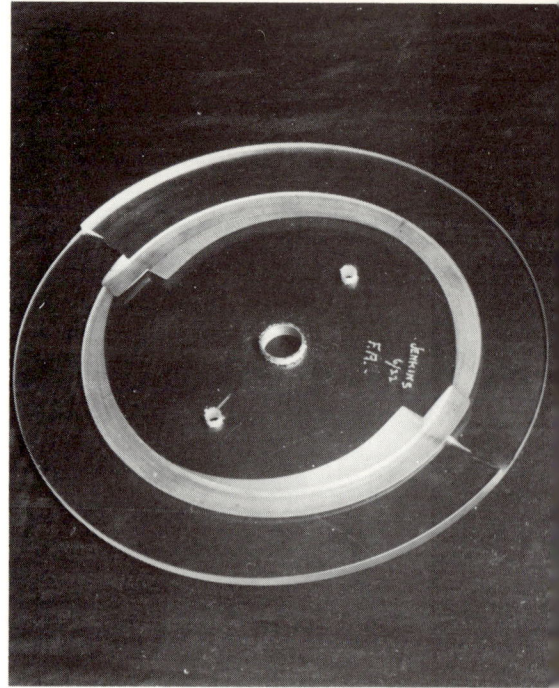

Above C F Jenkin's prismatic discs.

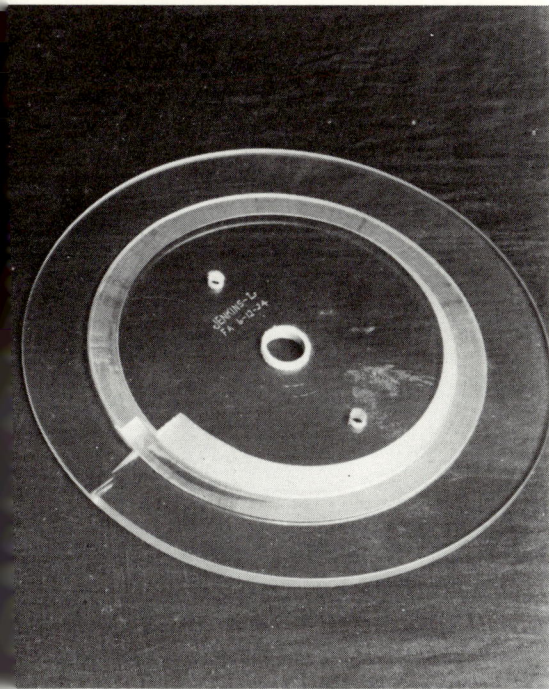

To Baird, however, the journey had not been entirely wasted. He had impressed on America the position of Britain in the development of television though he was naturally disappointed that his equipment could not be used there. There were at this time some experimental stations in America using 45-line and 60-line scanning systems and he would dearly have loved to add a Baird station to them. However it was not to be.

Another important thing happened to him in New York. Quietly and without fuss, on 13th November, 1931, at the Waldorf Hotel he married Margaret Albu, a concert pianist whom he had met in England the previous August.

When Baird returned from America events in the television field were moving fast. C F Jenkins in America was working on similar lines to Baird and using the Nipkow disc principle. He was getting on well and Baird knew that he was a serious rival. He was only a little behind and Baird knew that he must work hard and fast to keep ahead. In England the Marconi Company appeared on the scene as a rival but its interest was in transmitters rather than in cameras. Giant strides had been made in America by Westinghouse, AT&T and the Radio Corporation of America. In Germany the Post Office had made some successful experimental broadcasts and work was going on in France, Austria and other countries. Baird's hold on the world lead in mechanical television was slender but in the long run a much more serious threat to Baird's work was beginning to take form and substance—electronic television.

The germ of the idea of using electrons to make television work goes back to the theories of a great Scottish electrical engineer, A A Campbell Swinton, who published his first ideas in 1908. In those days however he could not see the practical detail of how his theory could be turned into working television. The receiver side was fairly straightforward, for cathode ray tubes of the type needed were already in use. In Russia in 1907 Boris Rosing had already demonstrated a crude television system using a mechanical camera and a cathode ray receiver. The real difficulty lay in the camera and Campbell Swinton could not see how this could work in practice. He set out his ideas in a letter to the scientific journal *Nature* which was published on 18th June, 1908. He concluded by saying, "Possibly no photo-electric phenomenon at present known will provide what is required in this respect, but should something suitable be discovered, distant electric vision will, I think, come within the region of possibility." His problem was how to turn the light and shade of the picture into a pattern of electrical signals.

Campbell Swinton's ideas were to be proved right but he was a long way ahead of his time. It was to be more than twenty years before scientists in their laboratories could turn his ideas into a working system, but when the breakthrough finally came electronic television arrived just as he had foreseen so long before.

Boris Rosing was the first man ever to demonstrate television of a sort. He could only show simple black and white outlines with no light and shade and the object had to be kept still in front of the camera, for if it moved at all the picture on the receiver broke up into squiggles. Nevertheless it was a start. Rosing was a Professor in St Petersburg, now Leningrad, in Russia. One of his students was a man called Vladimir Zworykin. When the Russian revolution broke out in 1917 Zworykin emigrated to America. He was keenly interested in electronics and while he was working for the great Westinghouse Corporation he found the solution to the problem of the electronic camera. In 1923 he filed an application for a patent for his camera that he called the "Iconoscope". There was still a long way to go, however, for at this stage he had only ideas of how to do it on paper. A lot

Right A A Campbell Swinton's scheme of 1912. The receiver end, with its cathode ray tube, was straightforward, but he knew he needed a plate which would turn the picture into electric signals. At that time an electronic camera had not been invented.

Right The Iconoscope made by V K Zworykin in 1931. You can see the square plate that converted the light into an electrical pattern.

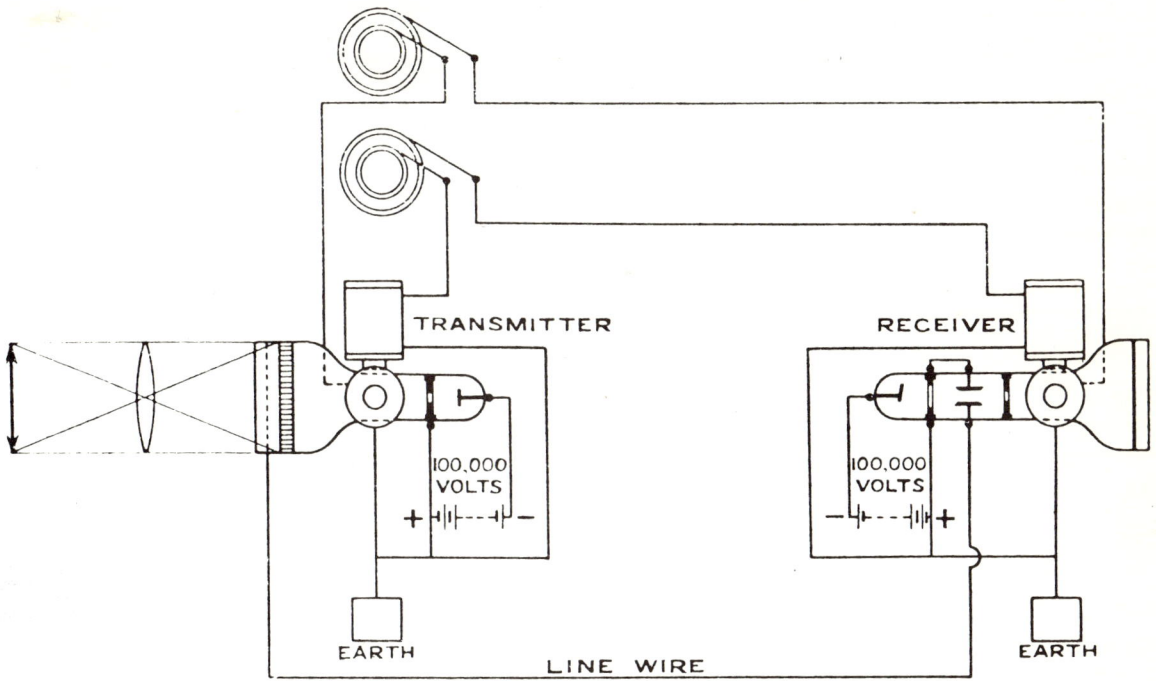

TRANSMITTER   RECEIVER

100,000
VOLTS

100,000
VOLTS

EARTH   LINE WIRE   EARTH

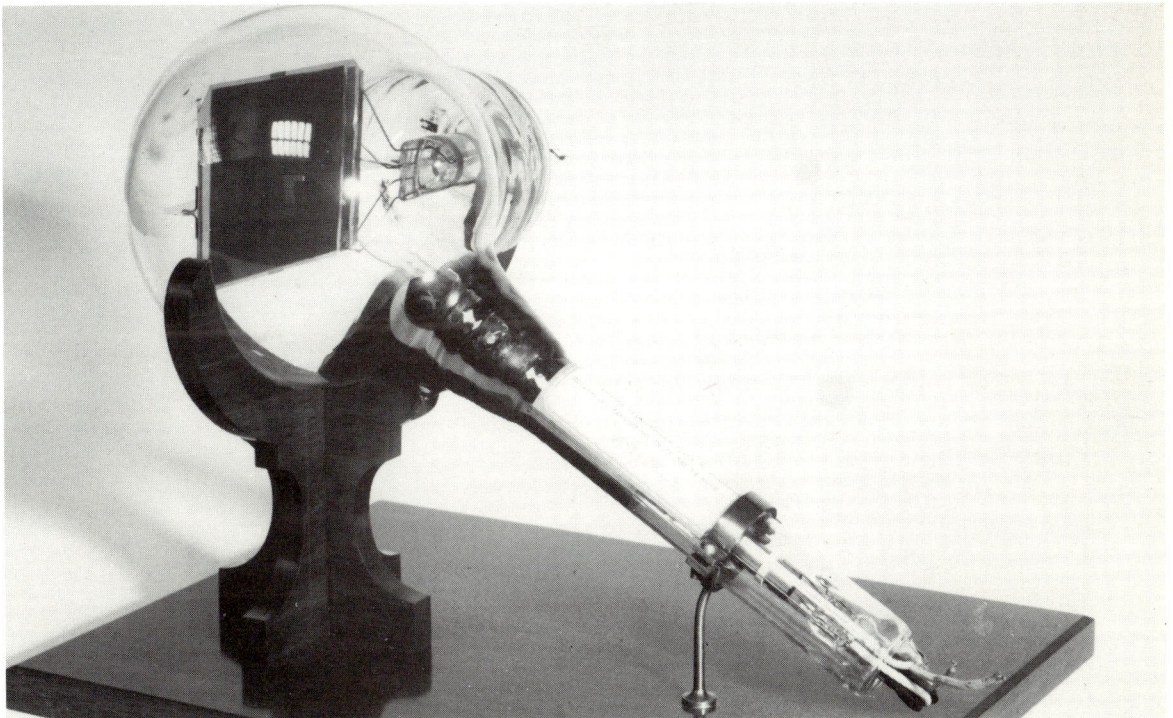

of practical work would have to be done before a working camera could be made. He did not have much in the way of facilities until he changed jobs and moved to another great American company, RCA. He made several Iconoscopes that worked but he was never satisfied. When he made each new tube he could see ways to improve it and he delayed completing his patent application time and again while he made yet more improvements. That is how it came about that although he was the first man to solve the riddle he was not the first man to patent an electronic television camera.

Events moved fast in England. In 1930 The Gramophone Company merged with others to form Electrical and Musical Industries, EMI for short. This company decided to go into television in a big way and to lead their research they appointed the brilliant scientist Isaac Schoenberg. He was also a Russian and had studied at St Petersburg though not at the same time as Zworykin. Schoenberg gathered an outstanding team who between them made many important advances in both radio and television. Two of the team went to America and met Zworykin and it seems likely that they picked up some useful tips, though nothing is officially recorded. Research at EMI moved swiftly on the camera tube and on the complicated circuits needed to make the complete camera. In only two years the job was done and EMI was granted a patent for its electronic camera tube, called the "Emitron". The Emitron was in principle very similar to Zworykin's Iconoscope, but there were important differences in the way that they were made. Soon the EMI engineers teamed up with the Marconi Company, whose knowledge of radio transmitters was unrivalled and between them they were able to produce the complete system from the studio camera to the transmitter. Not many people realised it in 1932, when Baird was at the height of his fame, but this development spelled the end of mechanical methods of television. For five years the two rival systems battled for supremacy, but the victory of the electronic scheme could not be long delayed.

1931 saw great strides. While Baird was working on the new mirror drum camera that he proposed to use to televise the Derby, news was coming in of successes all over the world. In America the RCA Corporation among others was making rapid progress. Telefunken in Germany was coming on fast and work was in progress in Austria and France. Baird worked on undeterred. No sooner was his Derby success over than he achieved another milestone: on July 14th he broadcast the world's first television play. It was *A Man with a Flower in his Mouth* by Pirandello and it was produced in Baird's Long Acre studio and transmitted by the BBC. It had a cast of two and there were no long shots, just two heads and two voices. This was very crude by our standards but compared to the sort of material that had been broadcast so far, it was a great leap to produce a whole play running for half an hour. Baird's drive and imagination had produced another milestone.

Until now Baird had been broadcasting on medium wave frequencies and this had two drawbacks. Firstly, these frequencies were becoming

Below An early Emitron camera tube.

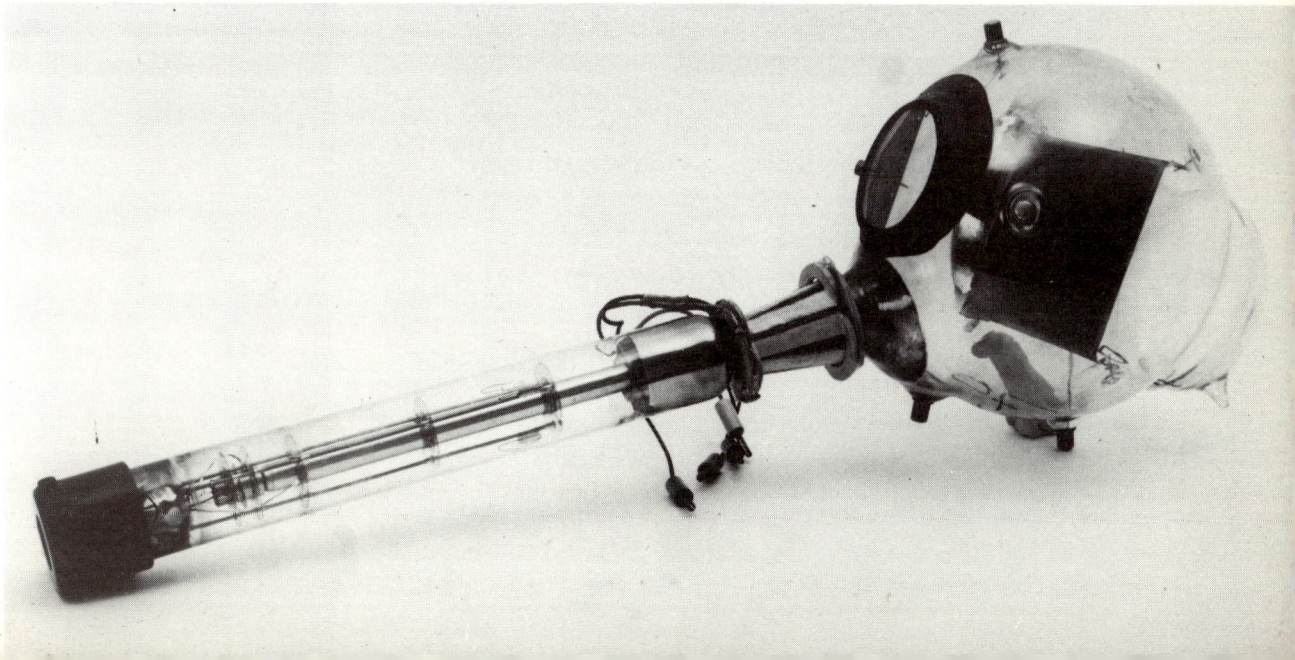

crowded with radio stations. Apart from the BBC there were many stations in other countries whose programmes could be heard in Britain. Radio Luxembourg had only just started with a small station; Radio Normandy was probably the station with the biggest audience. Radio Paris, Radio Hilversum, Radio Athlone and several others could all be received. These stations did a thriving business broadcasting English programmes sponsored by British advertisers, for the BBC would not accept any form of advertising. By 1934 British business was spending nearly a quarter of a million pounds on advertising, and in those days that was a large sum, and more and more stations grew up to meet the demand. It was almost like a rehearsal for the pirate radios of the 1960s.

The other drawback to medium waves was that television, which has to put over much more information than a sound programme because it has to include the picture details as well, needs a much wider "spread" of frequencies than a sound station. It was getting more and more difficult to find a big enough space in the crowded medium wave band to fit in a television transmitter. The solution was to move to a higher frequency into the short wave part of the range, where there were no stations broadcasting and the air was free and uncluttered. Technically it was difficult to produce a system that would work at high frequencies and nobody had tried it before so there was no experience to draw on. Typically, Baird pioneered the job himself and nobody who knew him was in the least surprised when he succeeded. He now had the "elbow room" among the radio frequencies to try to get more information into the picture signal and so get a sharper and clearer image. As usual Baird was quick to announce and demonstrate the step that he had taken, which he did at Gordon Selfridge's store in Oxford Street in April 1932.

The BBC was now becoming more enthusiastic.

Above Baird's mirror drum receiver of 1932, built by Bush. The picture was made of 30 lines, scanned vertically by mirror drum.

There were still many doubts about the clumsy apparatus and the dim and flickering pictures but there were many who saw the exciting prospect of a nationwide television service. They knew that technically there was a long way to go but they could also see where the road was leading. Baird had already built a camera for them. This was a mirror drum machine working on the "flying spot" system. The studio was like a vision from a bad dream. The great camera crouched in the dark and tall banks of photo-electric cells stood round it. The whole scene was lit only by the small but brilliant spot of light as it raced across the scene. Now the BBC was ready to move forward and on 22nd August, 1932 it took over programme production itself.

The race was now on for better and better definition, Baird striving to improve his mechanical means while Marconi-EMI had started work on their electronic system. Each in his own way tackled the same problem. The more lines into which you divide the picture the clearer the result will be. Baird had worked for some time on the basis of 30-lines per picture and had worked up to 60-lines but he had to go further—much further. His difficulty was a mechanical one, for on the mirror drum system you need one mirror for each line. To improve the picture more mirrors must be crowded round the edge of the drum. Each mirror had to be held exactly in place but as the drum was spinning fast there was a great force tending to throw the mirrors off. Frequently mirrors would be pushed out of place and the camera would have to be stopped while they were screwed back and cameramen who used these machines still remember their anxiety that they might be hit by a flying piece of glass. Fortunately however there is no record of anyone having been hurt. Despite the problems Baird steadily improved his cameras, first to 120-lines and finally to 240-lines. The solution to the problem of cramming in so many mirrors was to build them into a spiral, like a spiral staircase with the vertical part of each step being a mirror. In this way 240 of them could be fitted into a conveniently sized camera. One man who used this kind of camera was Douglas Birkinshaw, who later rose to become Chief Engineer—Television. He remembers them fondly and says that they could give a good steady picture.

Marconi-EMI also had their successes. Using the enormous speed at which electrons travel they were able to make a camera that could scan the picture area fifty times a second, twice as fast as was needed. Using this fact they were able effectively to double their basic system of 202·5-lines. The first scan would trace out the old-numbered lines, one, three, five, seven and so on. The next scan was shifted down a fraction so as to fill in the gaps by tracing out the even-numbered lines, two, four, six, eight etc. Thus in each 0·04 of a second the picture was scanned twice, giving in effect 405-lines.

Yet another rival appeared on the scene, HMV. They scored sufficient success for the BBC to take a close look at what they could do but Baird was not unduly worried. His move to higher frequencies was paying off and he was producing brighter and sharper pictures than ever before. He was working as hard as ever and, content now to leave the business side of affairs to his colleagues, his every thought was bent on television. Ideas flowed from him and he worked his staff harder and harder, but success came steadily. His pictures became steadier, sharper and brighter. He was confident that he could beat his rivals but at this stage he perhaps did not fully appreciate the danger that was developing for him in the electronic system. Whatever quality EMI could produce with their electronic cameras Baird could match with his mechanical methods. The BBC offered Baird a three-month trial of his new high frequency system and HMV dropped out of the run-

66

Above right An early Marconi combined television and radio receiver—the Marconiphone.

ning. The two great rivals once again had the field to themselves.

The Government meanwhile was watching from the sidelines. Experimental broadcasts had been going on for several years and it was clear to the staff at the Post Office that some day soon somebody would want to move on from occasional experiments to something more definite and regular. They could see, as the BBC could, that the possibility of a national television series was getting closer. When the time came the Cabinet Minister, the Postmaster General, would have to consider how to license it. The public was keenly interested too and the number of receivers in use was rising steadily. The original Baird "Televisor" went out of production in 1932 and more sophisticated machines based on the mirror-drum principle were being sold. At first Baird designed the receivers and got outside companies, including Bush, to produce them, but later of course his own company started to make them. However, a television set in those days was a much simpler thing than a modern set and large numbers of enthusiasts were building their own. With growing public enthusiasm and steadily improving results from the broadcasters the time had come to act. The first thing that the Postmaster General had to do was to decide which of the two great rival systems to use. To help him decide he set up a Royal Commission under Lord Selsdon to take a really close look and recommend which should be chosen. While the Commission criticized his pictures for looking a bit brownish but he cheered up when he heard that they had fought for, for so many years, the result of all the hardship, struggle and poverty that he had gone through, was now on trial but he never doubted that he would win.

Baird arranged demonstrations of his system in Wardour Street in Soho and Marconi-EMI set up their equipment nearby in Baker Street. He was a little downhearted when members of the Commission criticized his pictures for looking a bit brownish but he cheered up when he heard that they had criticized the Marconi-EMI results for looking a bit greenish. Then Baird went out to Crystal Palace, where he had his main laboratory, and there set up a demonstration of his big screen system. He had great difficulty in getting it right, and the lines that made up the picture showed clearly. When the members of the Commission arrived Baird was still unhappy with the equipment and behind the scenes he had several engineers constantly making adjustments to get the best out of it. Unfortunately someone noticed them and this spoiled the impression that he was trying to give. Months went by as the Commissioners argued, discussed and finally wrote their report. It was a time of great tension for Baird but there was nothing more that he could do. He mastered his impatience as best he could and got on with his work at the laboratory.

8 Setbacks

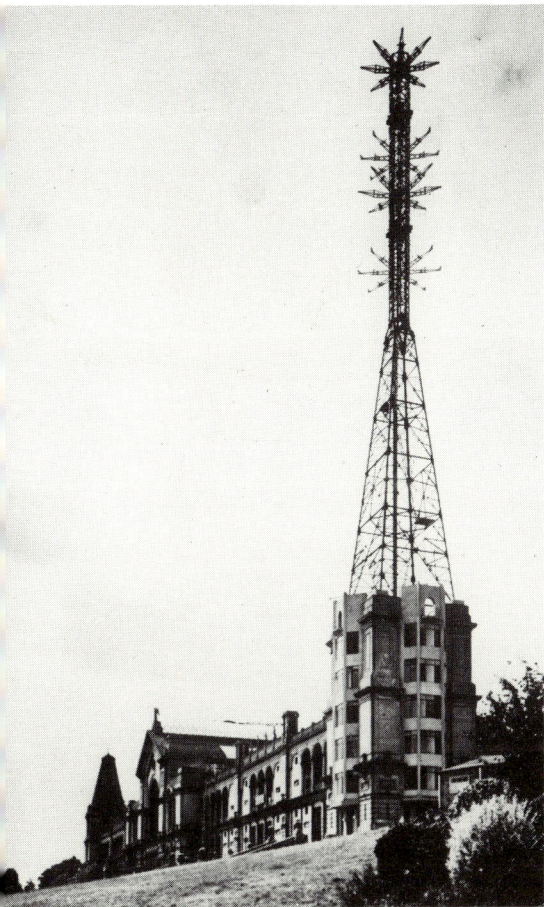

Below The first high-definition television station, at Alexandra Palace in 1936.

At last, in April 1935, the Selsdon Commission report was published. In a way it was an anti-climax. They had been asked to recommend which system should be officially adopted but they said it was too early, there was not yet enough experimental evidence to decide, and work should continue on both. However they did make two vital recommendations that were to shape television for a long time to come. Firstly they said the programmes should be produced by the BBC. This sounds simple, but the BBC already held the monopoly of sound radio and some people thought that to give them the television service would concentrate too much power in one place. Besides there were plenty of people, not least Baird himself, who were only too willing to make programmes. So the principle was established that television, like radio, should be in the hands of the BBC and paid for by licence fees. The second great recommendation was that the BBC should open as soon as possible a full-scale regular public television service on the highest standards available and use the Baird system one week and the Marconi-EMI the next, alternate them week by week so as to give them both a full public trial. Only after this had been done would enough be known about the merits of the two systems to make a choice.

The Government accepted this report and the BBC set to work at Alexandra Palace in North London. There was a great deal to be done to convert this large old building into a television centre. On the tower at the end of the building a tall steel structure was built to hold the transmitting aerials. Two studios had to be made, one for Baird and one for Marconi-EMI.

69

Above Baird's flying spot camera, 1935, in the control room at the BBC.

Transmitters were built, cameras and all the control equipment that goes with them were made and put in. Dressing rooms were needed for the artists and arrangements for making scenery. Lights, microphones and cables, chairs, tables, curtains, a whole host of details had to be organized and everything had to be thought up from scratch. There had never been a television service anywhere in the world and there was no experience to guide them. No one at this stage knew what the service would be like. What sort of programmes should they make and how? Under the guidance of Sir John Reith a small handful of men set to work to plan them, men like the engineers Birkinshaw and Bridgewater, and Cecil Madden, the Producer.

For Baird this was a hectic time at his laboratory at Crystal Palace. His flying spot cameras, which lit the subject by a small, brilliant and very fast moving spot of light, worked best with flat objects. It was not quite so successful with solid things in three dimensions. In order to achieve the sharpest possible picture Baird thought of a typically ingenious idea, the Intermediate Film Camera. This was an ordinary cinema camera that photographed the scene. The film went straight from the camera to the baths of processing chemicals. By keeping these chemicals hot the time needed to develop the film could be cut down to about

Below A broadcasting session at the Baird studio, Alexandra Palace, in August 1936.

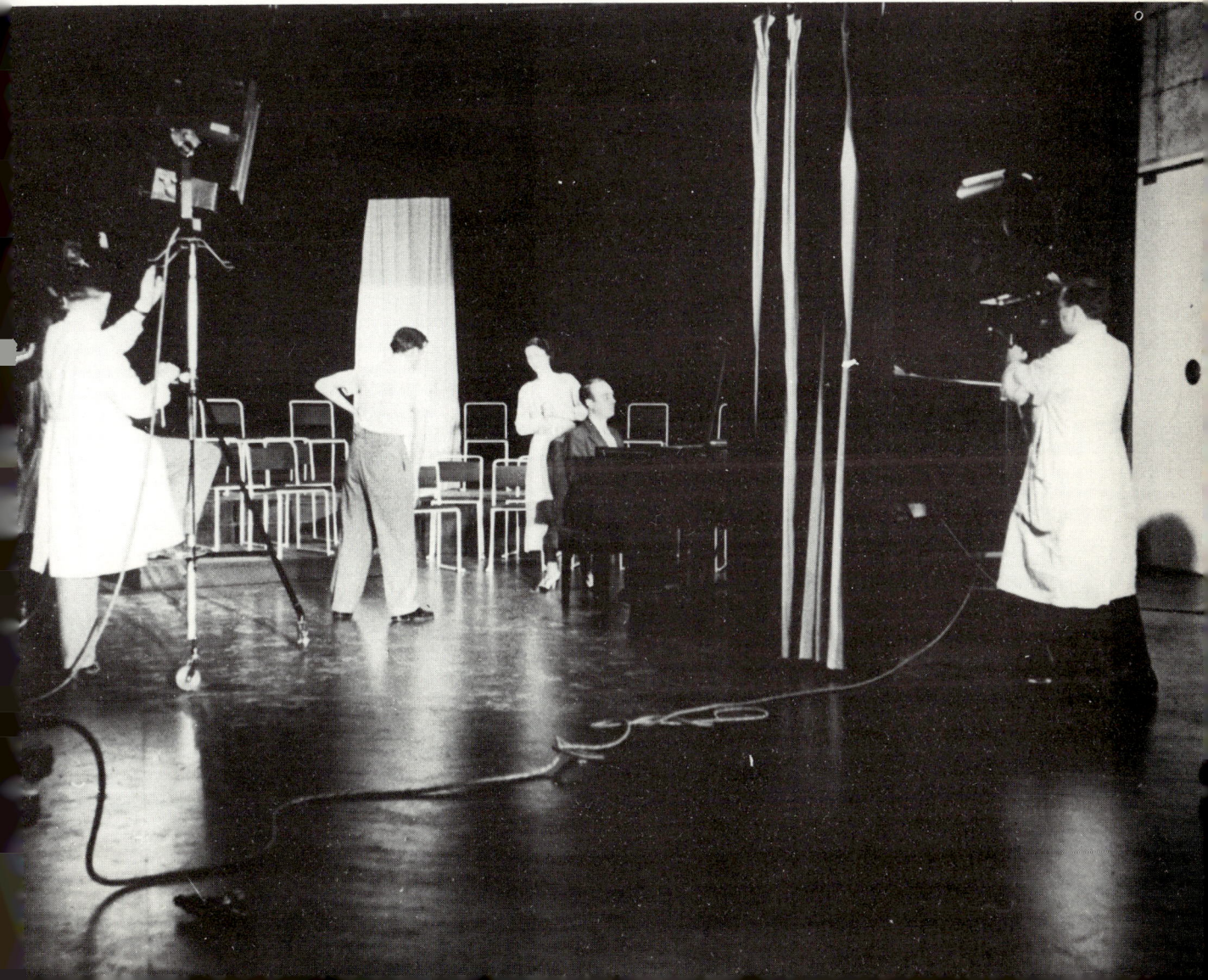

three minutes. The film, still wet, was then passed in front of the television camera. The result was a big, clumsy machine that had to be bolted to the studio floor but it did give a very good picture. It caused a lot of amusement as Alexandra Palace because of the delay between taking the picture and the television signal coming out at the end. An artist could perform in front of the camera and then have time to go round to the back and watch himself on television three minutes later. This complicated machine had to be designed and built, thoroughly tested and installed in the Baird studio at Alexandra Palace, so Baird and his helpers were kept very busy in the laboratories through the winter of 1935.

Before all was ready at the BBC an important series of broadcasts took place in Germany. The Olympic Games were held in Berlin in August 1936 and the whole proceedings were broadcast by the German Post Office, using mirror drum cameras similar to Baird's. After the Games, however, television in Germany closed down and did not start up again for some years. That is why Britain and John Logie Baird can fairly claim to have opened the world's first regular public television service.

At last the great day arrived and at 3.00 p.m. on Monday, 2nd November, 1936 the Postmaster General rose before Baird's camera to declare the service open. Baird himself was hot and uncomfortable in his smart suit and he tried to keep his unruly hair in order, but if he was nervous he did not show it. He had no need to worry. He and his colleagues had done their work well and the occasion was a triumphant success.

Although this was the first giant stride, steps were being taken in many places. Two months before the German broadcast of the Olympic Games, the National Broadcasting Company in America had opened an experimental electronic studio in New York, working with RCA. The studio was in the

Right The control room at Alexandra Palace television station—the Baird control desk for sound and vision.

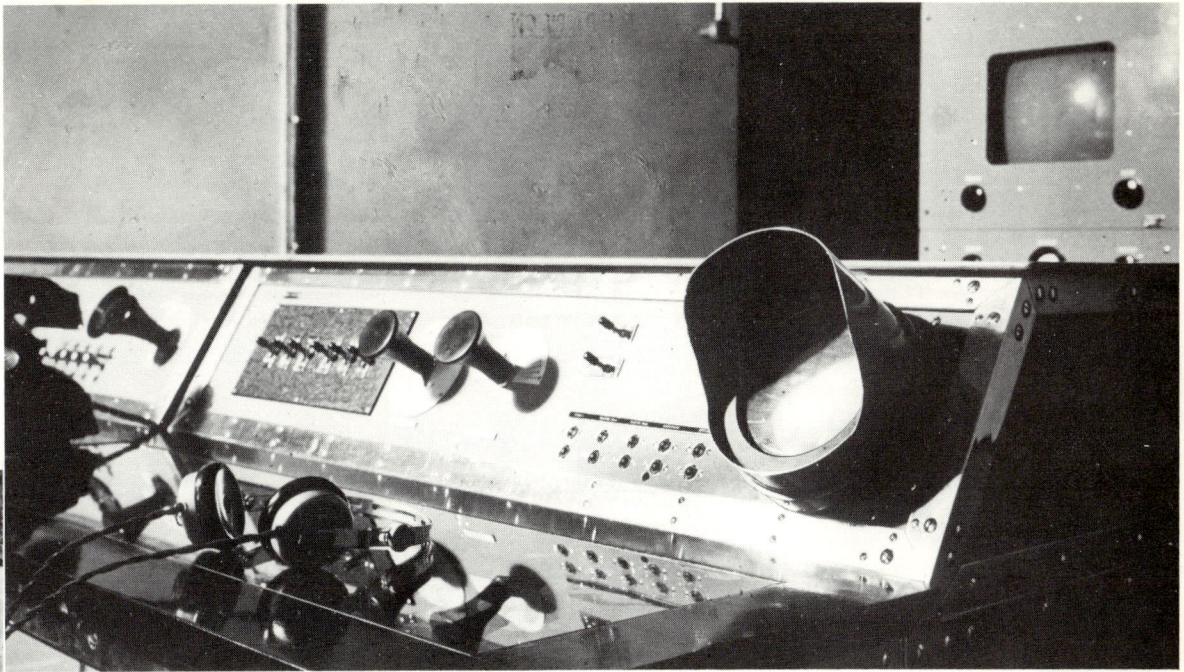

Left Baird with his sister Annie, in January 1937.

RCA buildings and the transmitter in the famous Empire State skyscraper. This studio broadcast was on 343-lines while British service used 405, but by the end of the year it had been improved to 441-lines.

As the year 1936 drew to its close Baird enjoyed the triumph for which he had struggled so hard and so long. Television had come to be as he foresaw ten years before. Then, still weak from his long illness, he had first started to experiment in Hastings with knitting needles and the lid of an old hat box. His success however was to be short lived. The man who all his life had been dogged by ill-health and bad luck was to be struck yet again. A disastrous fire broke out at Crystal Palace. It raged for a long time and when at last it was over the whole building was reduced to a tangled mass of iron. Baird's laboratory was utterly destroyed. All his valuable research equipment, plans, designs and drawings were gone. With his laboratory gone he had the greatest difficulty in maintaining the equipment at the BBC and this caused difficulties between him and the Corporation. Worse was yet to come. Although the quality of the pictures that came from Baird's cameras was good the big clumsy machines bolted to the studio floor could not compete with the light, mobile Emitron cameras on their wheeled dollies. In engineering circles they thought that although there was little to choose between the systems in terms of picture quality, the electronic system had the greater potential for future development. In February the following year the blow fell. It was announced in Parliament that the Marconi-EMI system had been chosen and Baird's mechanical television would be closed down forever. All Baird's great work lay in ruins. He was out of the BBC, he had not got into America. He felt bitter frustration as he went home to his wife at their house in Sydenham. Later he spoke with much gratitude of the support and encouragement she gave to him in this difficult time.

Disaster and Baird were no strangers. Several times before he had seen his successes ruined. He had never let it beat him before and he was not the man to be kept down for long even by so great a blow as this. He was soon back in London bubbling with ideas and fighting for them.

Since he no longer had a place in broadcast television, Baird reasoned that his future must lie in big-screen television in cinemas and theatres. He argued for a long time with the Directors of Gaumont-British cinemas, who had a big stake in his company. The equipment was already installed in the Dominion Theatre in Tottenham Court Road, so why not extend the system to all the other Gaumont-British cinemas? Instead of the weekly filmed Newsreels why not show events live, as they happened? The Directors were not convinced. It might work for a while but they thought that there was no future in it. Television was spreading fast and if the BBC could bring events live into the home why should people go out to the cinema to see them? He could not persuade them and they

Below Baird Model T5 set, made in 1937. Receiver tubes at this time deflected the cathode ray beam through only a narrow angle. A tube with a large face was very long and had to be mounted vertically.

Above Crystal Palace before it was destroyed by fire in 1936. Here Baird kept a lot of equipment—which was lost in the fire.

believed that the only thing that could be saved from the wreck of Baird's Company was the making of television sets. This side of the business was expanded and became successful. Baird television sets were among the best that you could buy but Baird himself took no interest because they were electronic and did not use his system.

Although he could not convince Gaumont-British, his old friend Isidore Ostrer caught his enthusiasm for big-screen television and together they set up a company, Cinema Television Ltd to exploit it. Baird was President and his invaluable business friend Moseley was on the Board. There was a bit of a row between Baird and Ostrer over the name of the Com-

Above The Baird large-screen television equipment at the Dominion Theatre, Tottenham Court Road, in 1935.

pany. Baird wanted his own name in it, after all it was a name that everyone knew. Ostrer insisted that the Company must not be tied down to any one system but remain free to take up any better one that should come along. The matter was settled in a friendly way and Baird happily set to doing what he liked best, developing equipment. He turned one room of his house in Sydenham into a laboratory and settled down to improve the big-screen system. Results came quickly. He was able to produce clearer, more sharply defined pictures and he found ways of over-

Above An Outside Broadcast by the BBC in June 1938. This was the first time that the Trooping of the Colour ceremony had been televised.

coming the flicker that had made his earlier efforts a strain to watch. Ostrer was delighted with progress and Baird dreamed of the day when the great sporting events could be seen as they happened in every cinema in the country. The warnings of Gaumont-British however were coming true. The BBC by now had Outside Broadcast units and regularly broadcast horse races, cricket matches and state occasions such as Trooping the Colour.

The Baird Company was prospering and its television sets were selling well. As Baird had his salary he was able to work on a number of projects in his laboratory. He was interested in the idea of three-dimensional television, and in colour television. He had already invented a mechanical colour system but could he work out a way of doing it electronically? He worked quietly and steadily, not saying much about what he was doing. In the early days his determination to keep Britain first in the field had driven him to demonstrate his ideas in public as soon as they could be made to work. He did not feel this pressure now and his life ran more smoothly. He made some progress with three-dimensional television and by 1938 he had dropped his earlier ideas for big-screen television using thousands of tiny electric light bulbs and instead had perfected an electronic television projector that would throw its picture onto the cinema's ordinary screen.

When Baird visited the Radio Show at Olympia in August 1939 he found great crowds as the public flocked to see the show. Baird receivers were selling like hot cakes but fate had yet another blow in store for him. The war broke out the next month and the television service was promptly closed down because the signals from a television transmitter would have been a great help to enemy bombers, who could use them to find their way. The closure was a disaster for Baird because no more sets were sold and the factory had to be closed down. Baird kept on a few of the staff out of his own pocket but there was little that he could do, for his own money was running out.

The Bairds now had two children and because of the risk of air raids they decided that Margaret should take them for safety to Bude in Cornwall. Baird stayed on in Sydenham with two assistants and visited his family when he could. Meanwhile he tried to find some work in which he could help the war effort. His health ruled out any active service but there would be a vast need for wireless and surely there was something that he could do. He wrote letters, visited people and telephoned his friends—but nobody seemed to want his services.

He carried on as best he could in his laboratory but money was short. The house was bombed and some of his equipment was damaged but he patched it up somehow and carried on in the undamaged part of the house. Here he succeeded in one of the tasks that he had set himself, electronic colour television. He had made a two-colour camera that he called

Above right An Outside Broadcast from Wembley stadium in April 1938.
The King is arriving for the Cup final.

Below right An early Outside Broadcast. The Arsenal team inspect the camera.

"Telechrome" and he patented this in the winter of 1940. For a while he was excited; when the war was over surely he could sell his new invention and his fortune would be made. In 1941 he invited the press to a demonstration of colour television. The journalists were very impressed but hardly a line about it appeared in the papers the next day for they were full of war news.

Moseley had gone to America at the outbreak of war and Baird wrote to him there because his Company had been wound up and he had no salary. Moseley replied at once, inviting Baird to bring his family over to America and continue his work on colour. He was reluctant to leave England and although he received several invitations to go to America, where his name still carried some weight, he could not make up his mind to go.

Baird became more and more withdrawn into himself. Money was a desperate worry for him. He had to sack one of his assistants and he could not go down to Bude to see his family as often as he would have liked because he could not afford the fare. When another bomb hit the house in Sydenham there was nothing he could do but mend the damaged equipment as best he could and carry on. Sometimes he was full of excitement, confident that his ideas would bring him success as soon as the war ended. At other times he would be full of despair, unable to see any way out of his worries.

His work still had its successes. One idea he was sure would succeed was a "Super TV" set with a giant screen three feet across. He designed this and wrote to Moseley to see if he could raise any backing in America to develop it. "Come over here," replied Moseley. "Demonstrate your set in America and you will get the backing you need." Still Baird would not leave. He struggled on, living in cheap hotels and going back every day to the damaged house at Syden-

Above right Baird's Telechrome tube.

Below right Baird holding his telechrome tube. This was a two-colour system, with one *electron-gun* for each colour.

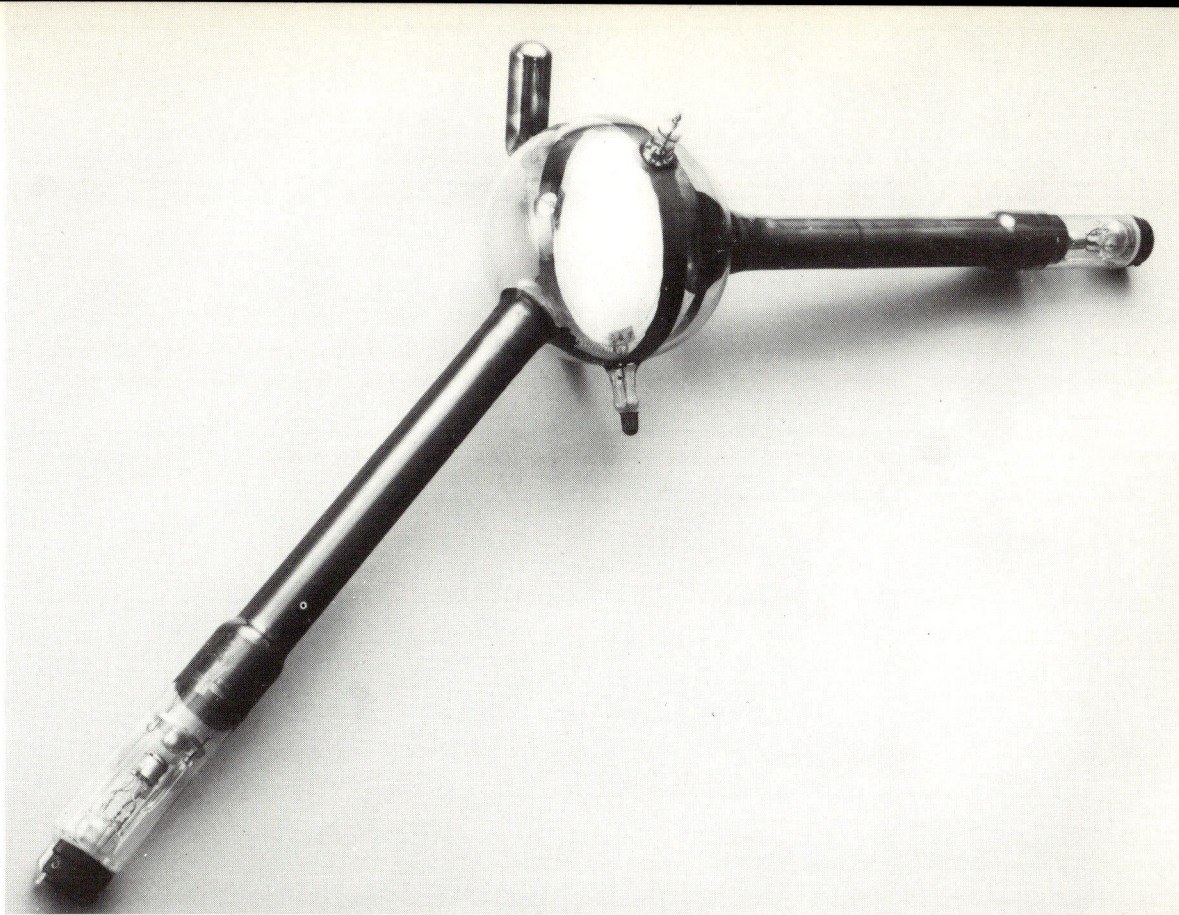

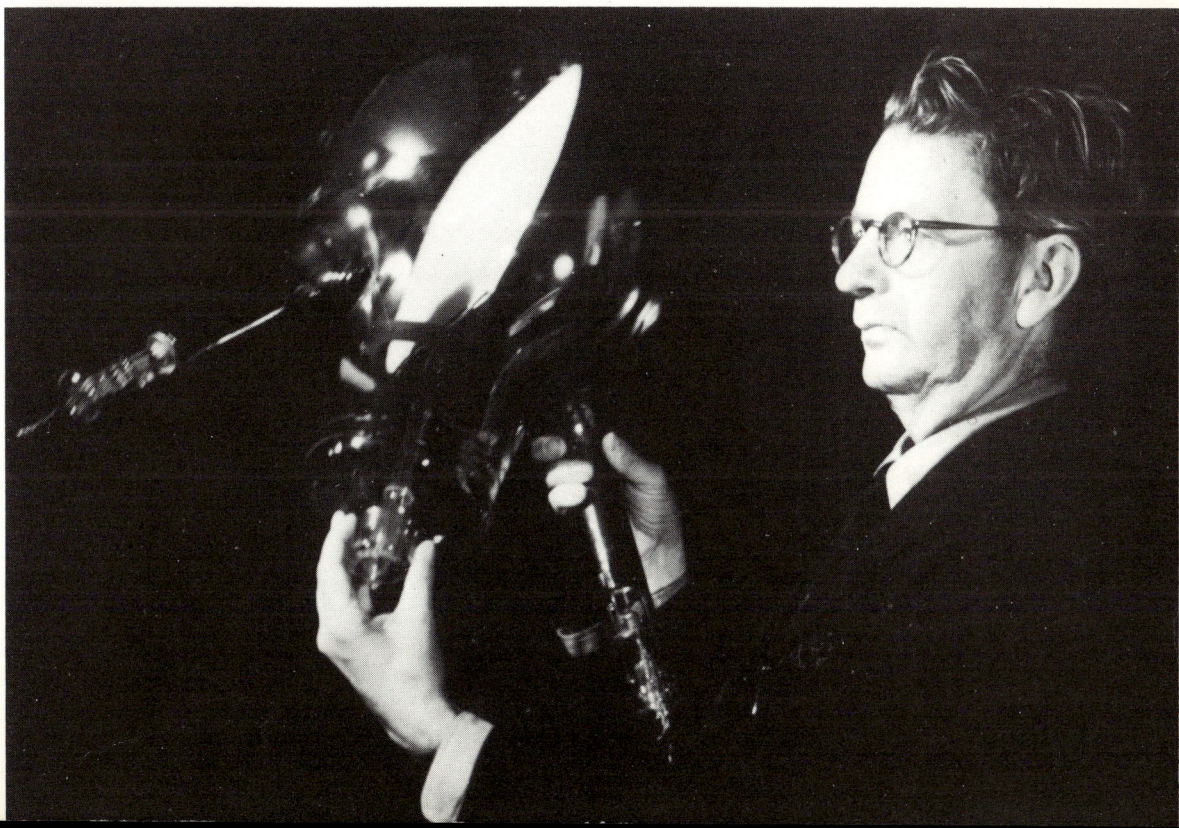

ham. Despite all the difficulties he continued to get results. He impressed the BBC very much by showing them colour television using 600 lines on a screen two and a half feet wide, but still he had no backing.

Moseley was getting more and more worried at the letters he was receiving from his old friend and when he had to come to England he took the opportunity to visit him. He was shocked to find Baird looking old, tired and ill. He seemed to have shrunk and although he was still quite young his face was lined and drawn. He could not afford his assistant but his work had to go on. If only he could survive through the war he was certain that at least his Super set would save him.

In the winter of 1945 Baird was struck by yet another of the desperately bad colds that had plagued him all his life. For a long time he lay ill but he did not give up, for it began to look as if the war was moving to its close. After the war, television would start again and he could get back to work. His Super set with its giant screen was ready; he could make it without a factory. He had had some success with three-D television, though little is known now of his ideas.

When the war was finally over Baird was full of impatience. At long last came the announcement for which he had waited for so many long, hard years. The BBC was to start its television service again in June 1946.

Baird was jubilant at the news. At last, he thought, his day had come. He set to work to tune his Super set and invited journalists to come and see the Victory Parades on television as it had never been seen before. All was set; but again fate struck and on the day of the demonstration Baird was taken ill, and his assistants had to demonstrate the set without him. The journalists were very impressed but tragically it was too late. This time it was not a heavy cold that had struck Baird down but pneumonia. A few days after the

Right D C Birkinshaw, later Chief Engineer—Television, behind the Marconi–EMI instantaneous camera in August 1936. Behind him is the television transmitting aerial.

demonstration he died, only fifty-eight years old.

His widow, who had nursed him devotedly through so many illnesses, took his body back to Helensburgh where he was born and there he rests.

Epilogue

So ended the story of John Logie Baird. What are we to make of this strange, heroic and tragic man who was one of the outstanding figures of the twentieth century? First, it is a story of almost unbelievable misfortune faced with extraordinary courage, persistence and determination. He must have been a good businessman, for how else could he have risen from each disaster to make the most of Baird socks, jam, soap and other ventures?

While it is not true to say that he invented television he was without doubt one of the most striking figures in the story and the part he played was a vital one, even though the system that he pioneered did not in the end succeed. The idea of television as we know it today we owe to A A Campbell Swinton. The solution to the problems raised by that theory we owe to Vladimir Zworykin in America and the first in the field was the brilliant team at EMI led by Isaac Schoenberg. But,.and here lies Baird's real importance, it was a very long step from Zworykin's solution to the factory-produced electronic cameras. To take that step big companies had to invest large sums of money and a lot of time. It was a big risk for them to take and at first Zworykin was unable to get the backing that he needed to develop his equipment. It was Baird who led the way, it was he who caught the

Right Report in the *Illustrated London News* of September 1926 of Baird's inventions.

TELEVISION: A NEW RADIO "MIRACLE"—THE TRANSMISSION OF PICTURES.

DRAWN BY OUR SPECIAL ARTIST, G. H. DAVIS, FROM SKETCHES OF THE ACTUAL APPARATUS AND INFORMATION SUPPLIED BY THE INVENTOR, MR. JOHN L. BAIRD.

THE LARGE LENS DISC IN THE TRANSMITTING STATION.

A.C. Synchronising motor.

Switch and control boards.

Operator's "television" for checking of electric signal being sent.

THE "TELEVISOR" EXPERIMENTAL TRANSMITTING STATION—2 TV.

Transmitters station.

The rapidly revolving lens disc.

Light-sensitive cell which varies the current in proportion to the light falling upon it.

Open end of box.

Amplifiers.

Motor.

Case.

Slotted disc revolving at high speed, which interrupts the light reflected from the image, causing it to reach the light-sensitive cell a series of flashes.

The cell then transmits a pulsating current of varying intensity.

Belt wheel.

Before reaching the cell the light passes through this rotating spiral slot, giving further subdivision of the image.

Receiving cell.

Belt driving spiral disc.

Power unit driving screw.

Receiving disc.

THE TRANSMITTERS STATION.

Bank of high power lamps.

Reflector.

Slot.

Side bank of lamps.

Microphone.

THE "TELEVISOR" HOME RECEIVING UNIT

Box containing filter circuit to separate the synchronous current from the current transmitting the image.

Amplifying valves.

"TELEVISOR" RECEIVING CABINET"

Receiving rotating shutter.

Alternating current synchronising motor, controlling motor driving rotating shutter. Both motors contained in one unit.

Loud speaker.

Box containing special type lamp lighted and controlled by the varying current.

Hand-controlled gear to focus image in centre of ground glass screen.

WIRELESS RECEIVING SET.

THE IMAGE AS RECEIVED

It is built up in a series of lines.

THE "TELEVISOR" RECEIVER IN USE.

Transmitted image on ground glass screen.

Controls.

G. H. DAVIS 1926

Above left Baird at the height of his fame in August 1932.

public imagination. It was he who got the press interested and sometimes excited. It was through his work that ordinary people began to see the intriguing possibilities of television. It was this fuse that Baird lit, this rising tide of interest in the press and in the public, that convinced the big companies, principally RCA in America and EMI in England, that there was a future for television. They would have to invest the money to develop it. If Baird had never existed, electronic television would have come in the end, but it is thanks to him that it came when it did. Without him we would have waited many more years.

Mr H J Barton-Chapple, an early colleague of John Logie Baird, adjusting the controls of a Televisor built in 1928.

Date Chart

1863	A A Campbell Swinton born.
	First still pictures were transmitted by wireless telegraphy in France.
1873	Joseph May discovered the properties of selenium when exposed to light.
1875	Bell invented the telephone, which led to numerous theoretical schemes for seeing by electricity.
1880	Isaac Schoenberg born.
1884	The Russian engineer Paul Nipkow patented his famous scanning disc in Berlin.
1888	John Logie Baird born.
	Professor Weiller demonstrated his mirror-drum scanner.
	Heinrich Hertz studied the nature of electro-magnetic waves.
1896	Guglielmo Marconi arrived in England and took out his first patent for a system of wireless telegraphy.
1897	Karl F Braun, of Germany, perfected a cathode ray display tube.
1901 (December 12)	Marconi, at Signal Hill, Newfoundland, received the first transatlantic wireless signal from Poldhu, Cornwall.
1906	Lee de Forest patented the Triode valve.
1907	In St Petersburg Boris Rosing demonstrated the use of the cathode ray tube as a television receiver, using a two mirror drum camera.

1908	A A Campbell Swinton wrote his famous letter to *Nature* in which he suggested the fundamental principles of modern electronic television. He concluded by saying, "Possibly no electric phenomenon at present known will provide what is required in this respect, but should something suitable be discovered distant electric vision will, I think, come within the region of possibility."
1918	Vladimir K Zworykin arrived in USA from Russia to work for Westinghouse.
1922	Baird went to Hastings.
1923	John Logie Baird started experiments in low-definition television. So also did C F Jenkins, who transmitted still pictures by wireless. Zworykin filed his patent application for a new camera tube, later called the Iconoscope. In Austria the Hungarian inventor Denes van Mihaly developed the "Telehor" which he claimed transmitted geometrical silhouettes.
1925	Baird set up in Frith Street, Soho.
(April)	Baird demonstrated his equipment at Selfridges in London, the first public demonstration of television.
(June)	In USA Jenkins gave one of the earliest demonstrations of low-definition television. His equipment showed the moving outline of a model windmill and was transmitted by wireless.
1926 (January)	Baird demonstrated his system to the Royal Institute.
(December)	Demonstration of "Noctovision".
1927 (April)	Television images were transmitted by

wire between New York and New Jersey by Bell Telephone Laboratories. Long Acre studios set up.

1928	Signal transmitted across the Atlantic.
1929	In London the BBC and the Baird Television Company commenced the regular experimental transmission of low-definition pictures on a 30-line system.
1930	The first receiving sets were sold in London, costing £18. A serious study of television was begun in Britain by the Gramophone Company.
1931 (September)	Baird sailed for New York.
	Baird televised the Derby.
1932	EMI patented the Emitron.
1935	Selsdon Commission Report.
1936 (2nd November)	Opening of BBC regular service.
1937 (February)	Mechanical TV closed down.
1940	"Telechrome" patented.
1946	Baird died.

Glossary

AMPLIFY   To increase the strength of an electric current.

AMPLIFIER   An arrangement of valves or transistors designed to increase power without losing the "pattern" of signal information.

CATHODE RAYS   Invisible rays given off by certain metals when heated in a *vacuum*. Some materials, called *phosphors,* glow when struck by *cathode* rays.

CATHODE RAY TUBE   A glass vessel in which electrical signals can be made visible by controlling *cathode rays* striking a *phosphor* screen, as in a television set. Alternatively a tube in which *cathode rays* are used to *scan* a thin film in which a pattern of light has been turned into an electrical pattern, as in a television camera.

ELECTRON   A minute electrically charged particle. Normally part of an atom, it can exist on its own in a *vacuum*.

ELECTRON GUN   A *vacuum* tube for producing streams of *electrons*.

LOUDSPEAKER   A device for turning an electrical signal into sound.

MICROPHONE   A device for turning sound into an electrical signal.

MOSAIC   An arrangement of light-sensitive particles used to translate light into electricity.

PHOSPHOR   A fluorescent substance that glows when struck by a stream of *electrons*.

PHOTO-ELECTRIC CELL   An instrument, originally made of *selenium,* which varies the amount of electricity flowing through it according to the amount of light that falls on it.

RESISTANCE   An instrument, usually of fine wire, to cut down the amount of electricity.

SCAN   To look at a picture a little bit at a time by sweeping it in a series of fine lines either mechanically or by *electrons*.

SELENIUM   A metal whose *resistance* to electricity varies with the amount of light striking it.

TELEGRAPH   A simple machine for sending signals by wire.

VACUUM   A space from which the air has been pumped out.

Further Reading

For a general discussion of the media, see
Talking about Mass Media, Catherine Baker (Wayland
    Publishers, 1973)

Two books about modern Broadcasting:
Television—Here is the News, Anthony Davies (Severn
    House Publishers, 1976)
Television—Behind the Scene, Peter Fairley (Severn
    House Publishers, 1976)

A history of television with many illustrations of popular programmes is
Do you remember Book—Television, Burton Graham
    (Marshall Cavendish Golden Hands Series, 1974)

Younger students will enjoy
Television, Keith Wicks (Macdonald Introduction to
    Technology Series, 1975)

For current information about Independent Television and Independent Local Radio, try the annual handbook
Television and Radio, (Independent Broadcasting
    Authority)

Index

Picture Credits

The author and publishers would like to thank all those who
have given permission for their illustrations to appear on the
following pages:
Barnaby's Picture Library: 75; Mr H J Barton-Chapple: 50;
The British Broadcasting Corporation: 6, 48, 70, 71, 73, 76, 77,
79 (both), 86; British Library Newspaper Library: 41; Celia
Ware: 32, 33, 45, 55 (both); The Independent Broadcasting
Authority, Broadcasting Gallery: 13, 26, 37 (left), 48–49,
52–53, 63, 64, 74, 81 (below) 87; Radio Times Hulton Picture
Library: Frontispiece, 9, 10, 22, 34, 37 (right), 42, 46, 51, 69,
72, 83; Science Museum: 11, 12 (both), 15, 16, 19, 31, 58–59, 61
(both), 67; Science Museum, Crown Copyright: 81 (above);
Strathclyde University: 22, 23, 25, 39, 56; Wayland Picture
Library: 18, 85.